Deepening The Commitment: Zionism and the Conservative/Masorti Movement

Deepening The Commitment: Zionism and the Conservative/Masorti Movement

Papers from a conference of Conservative/Masorti Movement Leadership held September 7–8, 1988 at The Jewish Theological Seminary of America, New York City

Edited by
JOHN S. RUSKAY
and
DAVID M. SZONYI

THE JEWISH THEOLOGICAL SEMINARY OF AMERICA
NEW YORK, 1990

Copyright ©1990
Jewish Theological Seminary of America

Deepening the commitment : Zionism and the Conservative/Masorti movement : papers from a conference of Conservative/Masorti movement leadership held September 7-8, 1988 at the Jewish Theological Seminary of America, New York City / edited by John S. Ruskay and David M. Szonyi.
    p.   cm.
    ISBN 0-87334-059-0
    1. Conservative Judaism—Israel—Congresses. 2. Israel and the Diaspora—Congresses. 3. Jews—United States—Attitudes toward Israel—Congresses. I. Ruskay, John S., 1946-   . II. Szonyi, David M. III. Jewish Theological Seminary of America.
BM197.5.D44 1990
296.8'342'095694—dc20   90-4208
                                                                                 CIP

Manufactured in the United States of America

This publication was made possible by the generous support of Harold B. Pressman who for more than forty years has been a leader of Conservative Judaism. Mr. Pressman served as a regional and national officer of the United Synagogue of America and co-chairman of the Seminary's National Enrollment Plan. He is a past president of Temple Sinai in Dresher, PA., and is currently vice-president of Congregation Bet Tikvah in Lake Worth, Fla., where he now resides with his wife, Selma Rapaport Pressman.

Contents

INTRODUCTION — *John Ruskay* ... vii

ACKNOWLEDGMENTS ... xiii

PLENARY ADDRESSES ... 1
  A Light Unto the Nations ... 1
    Ismar Schorsch
  Conservative Judaism and Zionism: Toward the Twenty-First Century ... 7
    Lee Levine

SEMINAR PAPERS

SEMINAR 1. DEMOCRATIC VALUES IN THE STATE OF ISRAEL ... 15
  Conservative Judaism's Role in Fostering Democratic Values ... 17
    Shoshana S. Cardin
  A Conservative-Masorti Perspective ... 25
    David Gordis
  Zionism, Democracy, and Judaism ... 33
    Barbara Spectre
  The Struggle for Democratic Values in the State of Israel ... 41
    Gad Ufaz

SEMINAR 2. ISRAEL–DIASPORA RELATIONS ... 51
  Conservative/Masorti Zionism in a Rapidly Changing World ... 53
    Raphael Arzt
  To Strengthen Weak Ties: The Conservative Movement and the Country of Israel ... 59
    Steven M. Cohen

Ways to Deepen Conservative "Israel Consciousness" *Paul Freedman*	67
The Ongoing Importance of the Diaspora *David Lieber*	71
SEMINAR 3. THE ROLE OF RELIGION IN ISRAEL	77
Strategies for the Conservative/Masorti Movement *Charles S. Liebman*	79
The Conservative Movement and Israel *Stanley Rabinowitz*	87
SEMINAR 4. ALIYAH	95
Aliyah: Abroad Thoughts from Home *Jac Friedgut*	97
Aliyah and Alternatives to Aliyah *Paula Hyman*	105
North American Conservative Judaism and Education *Benjamin Segal*	111
Eretz Yisrael and Aliyah: A Jewish Zionist View *Joseph S. Wernik*	119
SEMINAR 5. THE CENTRALITY OF THE STATE OF ISRAEL IN JEWISH LIFE	127
The Ambiguity of Our Ties to Israel *Neil Gillman*	129
The Task of Masorti Judaism *Moshe Greenberg*	137
The Actualization of the Traditional View of Israel's Centrality *Reuven Hammer*	147
SEMINAR 6. PEACE, LAND, AND SECURITY IN THE STATE OF ISRAEL	157
The Need for a New Zionism *Philip Spectre*	159
Israel—the Security Dilemma *Jacob Stein*	165
Israel Is Fighting for Her Life *Joseph P. Sternstein*	171
The Necessity of Aiding Israel's Progressive Elements *Leon Waldman*	179
Contributors	183
CONFERENCE PARTICIPANTS	189
CONFERENCE PROGRAM	195

Introduction

The Conservative Movement's identification with Zionism goes back virtually to the days of Theodor Herzl. With few exceptions, the movement's leadership supported the Zionist goal of creating a Jewish homeland in Palestine. However, despite its ideological identification with Zionism in the prestate period, Conservative Judaism did not take an active role in building the Jewish national home. Although the Seminary established a campus in Jerusalem in 1962, and the movement's youth arms, USY and Camp Ramah, brought hundreds of teenagers to Israel each summer, the movement's priorities were focussed on North America—to build synagogues, strengthen Jewish education, and embrace a broad range of programs to enrich Jewish culture and Jewish identity. As Chancellor Ismar Schorsch recently explained, the "ambivalence of the Seminary (and the movement) was on the whole not due to an opposition to Jewish nationalism or its political expression. During the 1950's and 1960's, the intellectual atmosphere of the Seminary (and the movement) was strongly oriented to creating a self-sufficient Jewish life in the Diaspora."

One significant exception was embodied in a small yet important cadre of Conservative Jews, primarily rabbis, who made aliyah and began to create a Conservative/Masorti Movement in Israel in the early 1970's. Their dual commitment to Zionism and Conservative Judaism was expressed in establishing synagogues, the NOAM Youth Movement (in the 1970's), the Association of Masorti congregations (founded in 1979), the Tali Schools (first established in 1976), and more recently Kibbutz Hanaton (1984) and an overnight Camp Ramah–NOAM (in 1988). These efforts were undertaken with important though modest financial support from North America.

By the late 1970's, aliyah by Conservative Jews had created a presence that was increasingly seen as an important investment of the movement in Israel. This changed perspective led to the creation in 1979 of the Foundation for Masorti Judaism in Israel to foster a strengthened Conservative presence in Israel. Support for the development of the Conservative/Masorti Movement grew when in 1984, with support from then Seminary Chancellor Dr. Gerson Cohen, the movement established in Jerusalem the Seminary for Judaic Studies (the Beit Midrash) to train Israelis as Masorti rabbis and educators in Israel.

The papers contained in this volume were presented at a two-day conference for the worldwide leadership of Conservative Judaism: "Zionism and Zionist Thought Within the Conservative/Masorti Movement: Deepening Our Commitment." It was held at the Seminary in September 1988. The conference represented another manifestation of the Conservative Movement's growing involvement in Zionism and support for Masorti Judaism in Israel. Convened by the Seminary Chancellor, Dr. Ismar Schorsch, in cooperation with the United Synagogue of America, the Rabbinical Assembly, the Women's League for Conservative Judaism, the Federation of Jewish Men's Clubs, the World Council of Synagogues, Mercaz, the Foundation for Conservative Judaism in Israel, the Masorti Movement, the University of Judaism, and the Seminary, the conference reflected the increased importance of Israel on the agenda of Conservative Judaism.

Since 1986, Chancellor Schorsch has vigorously led this effort to strengthen the movement's bonds with the Masorti Movement in Israel and to raise the level of support for it. As part of the celebration of the Seminary Centennial in 1986, a board mission traveled to Israel and conducted a meeting there for the first time. Chancellor Schorsch also led intensive efforts to involve the Conservative Movement in such international bodies as the World Zionist Congress. At the most recent World Zionist Congress (1987), a large Mercaz delegation was present as the Conservative/Masorti Movement assumed a significant role in the central body of international Jewish governance.

The first commencement of the Beit Midrash in July 1988 induced the United Synagogue of America and the Rabbinical Assembly to hold their international conventions in Jerusalem. The large attendance of movement leadership from abroad testified to the growing bonds between the North American and Israeli Conservative/Masorti Movements. Perhaps most important, from 1985 to the present, funding for the institutions and programs of the Conservative/Masorti Movement in Israel has grown over three hundred percent; movement leadership increasingly recognized that the growth of Masorti Judaism in Israel is indispensable to the future of Conservative Judaism internationally and contributes to the strengthening of religious pluralism in Israel and in the Diaspora.

In March 1988, the Conservative Movement produced its first statement of principles. Prepared by a movement-wide commission chaired by Professor Robert Gordis, *Emet v'Emunah* ("truth and faith") articulated the movement's ideology on a broad range of theological and social issues, including Zionism, religious pluralism in Israel, and Israel–Diaspora relations. While the publication of *Emet v'Emunah* was an important step toward providing concise movement perspective, the 1988 conference on "Zionism and Zionist Thought: Deepening Our Commitments" reflected a recognition that Conservative Jewry's leadership needed further ideological clarification if the programmatic expressions of support for the Masorti Movement in Israel were to be serious and sustained.

In elucidating the understanding of Conservative Jews on such central Zionist issues as the centrality of Israel, religion and state in Israel, Diaspora–Israel relations, democratic values in the State of Israel, aliyah, and peace, land, and security in the State of Israel, the movement's leadership sought to clarify its understanding of contemporary Zionism as Israel enters its fifth decade.

This volume contains the twenty-one papers presented at the six seminars on the first day of the conference. Also included are major plenary addresses presented by Chancellor Schorsch and Dr. Lee Levine, Seminary Vice Chancellor for Israel Affairs and Dean of the Seminary of Judaic Studies in Jerusalem.

The two days of discussion were intense, with broad consensus on numerous issues and sharp disagreement on others. However, in bringing together the leadership from all arms of Conservative Judaism throughout the world (see the list of participants in the Appendix), the conference helped them to begin the process of forging a new integration of contemporary Conservative Judaism and Zionism.

Prior to the establishment of the Jewish state in 1948, Zionism was characterized by intense ideological divisions. Adherents of the many Zionist movements had their own positions on the central issues concerning the character of the future Jewish national home. In identifying with a Zionist movement, one had to decide whether one favored a religious or secular state, a capitalist, socialist, or mixed economy, and even whether one favored the establishment of a distinctively Jewish or a binational state. Each of the movements and political parties had its own perspective on these (and other) issues, and therefore an individual's Zionist movement affiliation often reflected a serious position on the desired Jewish future.

With the state's establishment in 1948, this ideological debate ended while most Jews affirmed and celebrated the victorious synthesis of a secular Jewish state in a part of the Jews' ancient homeland. The end of a vigorous Zionist debate on fundamentals was essential as Israel faced the challenge of building a society in a hostile environment. However, the lack of ideological vigor and debate deprived a whole generation of the value of having to grapple seriously with the nature of one's Zionist commitments.

The Conservative Movement hopes that this volume will contribute to the challenge of forging a vibrant Zionist ideology for both Conservative Jewry and the broader community. It represents only the beginning of such an effort, as evidenced by the planning now under way for a second movement-wide conference.

It is the hope of all who labored to develop the conference and to prepare this publication that it will serve as a resource to "deepen our commitments" to Israel and Zionism. Recent events continue to underscore the interdependence of world Jewry. Israel's future and that of Diaspora Jewry are inextricably linked. Despite our internal disagreements, we are one people, with a shared history and destiny. May this volume contribute to the strengthening of all who share a commitment to building a democratic and pluralistic State of Israel.

John Ruskay

July, 1989

Acknowledgments

This volume, and the 1988 conference, "Zionism and Zionist Thought Within the Conservative/Masorti Movement: Deepening Our Commitments," is the product of an extraordinary collective effort within the movement.

As noted in the Introduction, the conference was co-sponsored by ten organizations. The conference committee designed the conference, ensuring the engagement of movement leadership from both North America and Israel, and determined all aspects of the conference. The effort was noteworthy both by the quality of committee involvement and the fact that virtually every arm of the movement participated actively. As Chairman of the Conference Planning Committee, I wish to acknowledge and thank those who served on the planning committee:

Tom Kagedan, Dr. Saul Shapiro	United Synagogue of America
Rabbi James Michaels, Rabbi Ezra Finkelstein	Rabbinical Assembly
Evelyn Auerbach, Bernice Balter	Women's League for Conservative Judaism
Joseph Gurmankin, Rabbi Charles Simon	Federation of Jewish Men's Clubs
Simon Schwartz, Hindy Kisch, Motti Arad	Mercaz
Neil Norry, Rabbi Michael Monson	Foundation for Conservative Judaism in Israel

Rabbi Philip Spectre	Masorti Movement (Israel)
Marshall Wolke, Bernard Barsky	World Council of Synagogues
Dr. John Ruskay, Dr. Steven M. Cohen	Jewish Theological Seminary
Dr. David Lieber	University of Judaism

A special word of thanks is due Renee Gutman, Director of the Seminary's Department of Public Events and Government Relations. Her many years of experience were enormous assets in making certain that conference arrangements, large and small, were superbly implemented. She received important assistance from Hindy Kisch, the Executive Director of Mercaz. Dr. Steven M. Cohen drafted the questions and issues, on behalf of the planning committee, which were presented in advance to those preparing papers and are included before each section of papers in this volume.

With the conference concluded, work immediately began on arranging for the publication of the conference papers. David Szonyi was engaged to both coedit the volume and coordinate the effort. While publications always appear later than some would hope, it is a testimony to Mr. Szonyi's editorial and managerial skills that this manuscript is complete eight months after the conference. Rabbi Charles Simon and Jean Highland provided important guidance in making the arrangements for publication.

The efforts of all of these individuals, as well as those who attended and participated in the conference, were energized by a shared commitment to the enterprise of deepening the understanding and commitment to contemporary Zionism and the challenge of developing a vital Zionist ideology for the Conservative Movement as it enters its second century. Future developments will enable us to assess the long-term significance of this effort. At present, I express our profound appreciation to all who contributed to the conference and the publication of this volume

J. S. R.

June 5, 1989

A Light Unto the Nations

ISMAR SCHORSCH

In February 1923, Albert Einstein gave the inaugural lecture of the Hebrew University on Mount Scopus. In his introductory remarks, Menahem Ussishkin spoke of the "lectern that had waited for him for two thousand years." On a smaller scale, the Zionist movement waited nearly nine decades before Conservative Judaism appeared at a Zionist Congress. What a sad and sensless delay. The founders of Conservatism were avowed Zionists before Herzl was born. Intrepidly, Zacharias Frankel and Heinrich Graetz defended the national character of Judaism. For them, Hebrew was a living language, the Jewish people a dynamic force, the land of Israel an object of longing, and exile a condition of Jewish existence fundamentally unchanged by emancipation. They railed against Reform because it so readily had betrayed the nationhood of Israel. Their courage, pride, and scholarship laid the seedbed for many a later Zionist.

Our collective debut in Jerusalem at the 31st Zionist Congress was respectable and influential. But the hype of a congress soon wears off. Our admission into the World Zionist Organization must require more of us than an ongoing concern for new members and an occasional election campaign. Through ongoing dialogue and deliberation, we must examine our views, share our unease, and give voice to our ideals. In short, we must add a vital dimension to Conservative Judaism's burgeoning presence in Israel.

What has prompted our Copernican turn to Zion, which may one day soon make Mercaz and Masorti Judaism household words within our movement? I believe there are at least four cogent reasons why we should be active in Israel on a large scale.

1. Israel embodies a unique historical achievement, which remains undimmed after forty years: the reversal of two millennia of national homelessness. The recovery of political sovereignty, in the very land in which it was lost to the Romans in 63 B.C.E. is a singular expression of unbroken historical consciousness steeled by religious faith. Israel's sterling record of commitment to democracy, absorption of refugees, social equality, agricultural development, scientific excellence, cultural creativity, and military prowess, achieved under the most adverse of conditions, is unmatched by any other state founded since World War II. For Conservative Jews, as heirs of the Historical School, it would be a travesty to observe from the sidelines this adventure in overcoming historical inertia and political difficulties.

2. Israel represents the most potent unifying force in a secular age in which the Jewish people have become deeply fragmented religiously. Israel stirs the emotions of secular and religious Jews alike, particularly in moments of crisis. According to Abraham Joshua Heschel, its very existence helped alleviate the anguish of the Holocaust: its stunning accomplishments inspired Diaspora Jews with awe, pride, and ethnic commitment.

Nothing endangers its centrality in Jewish life more gravely than the continued growth of Orthodox power in public life. Better to drop the Law of Return, once a symbol of Jewish unity, than to delegitimize the Reform and Conservative rabbinates of the Diaspora by amending it. Israel must not permit itself to be recast in the image of an East European shtetl. To prevent this nightmarish prospect, I call upon Israel's political leaders to mandate military service for all qualified yeshiva students and to require a university degree for all state rabbis and rabbinic judges. Insularity always has been the ideal breeding ground for religious folly and fanaticism.

3. We Conservative Jews are active in Israel to offer an alternative Judaism. The vast majority of Israelis are religiously disenfranchised, severed from their spiritual roots. To be sure, they are

secular in part by choice, but also in part by lack of choice. Few Jews would remain in the open societies of the United States or Canada were Orthodoxy the only religious option. The national definition of Israel as a Jewish state has concealed the disastrous failure of Orthodoxy to expose some eighty percent of Israel Jewry to even a modicum of religious vocabulary, study, and observance. The more introverted and coercive Israeli Orthodoxy becomes, the greater will be the alienation from it. Genuine religious pluralism is vital not only to improve Israel–Diaspora relations but also to reconnect Israeli Jews to Judaism. As shown by the inroads into Israeli society that we already have made, Conservatism is ideally suited for that historical task.

4. Our deepening involvement in Israel is motivated by a fear of political rupture. Since the Emancipation, the pervasive political ethos of modern Jewry has been democratic for very good reasons. The extension of varying degrees of equality to Jews in such countries as England, France, Prussia, and Russia always was related to a broader thrust to restructure the body politic. Thus advocates of Jewish emancipation never were found among the defenders of the old order. Not surprisingly, Jews aligned with the politics of their benefactors and embraced the vision of a free society based on the rule of law. Whatever their individual preference today, Diaspora Jews remain viscerally committed to the political culture of Western democracy.

The rising tide of contempt for democratic culture in certain right-wing Israeli circles (and among many young people) threatens the basic political concord between Israel and the Diaspora that has existed since the state's founding. This is especially the case if Meir Kahane and his ilk are saying what others merely think. Jews cannot denounce Jean Marie Le Pen in France and back Kahane in Israel. Such hypocrisy would repel Diaspora Jewry while mocking Israel's founders. To trifle with Israel's commitment to democracy is a Faustian gamble that will cost all Jews dearly.

The *intifada* erupted during the Zionist Congress in December 1987; it has yet to be quelled. Despite the media's merciless scrutiny, it has been handled in a way reminiscent of the Haganah's policy of *havlagah* (restraint) toward the Palestinian uprisings of the thirties, and with less brutality and bloodshed than usually mark the repression of a national rebellion. Still, the eruption is deeply troubling. Israel's fate hangs in the balance, and we should not be cowed by would-be voices of authority and expertise.

What is obvious is that the struggle has finally come down to one between the actual inhabitants of the land, the Israeli Jews and the Palestinian Arabs. The surrounding Arab states, which had led the battle against Israel since 1948, have withdrawn from the fray. Egypt settled for a separate peace after a semblance of victory in the Yom Kippur War. It has adhered to the peace treaty despite such Israeli provocation as the 1982 invasion of Lebanon. Jordan has maintained a peaceful border with Israel since at least 1970, when it drove out the PLO. Israel's invasion of Lebanon proved that Syria will not fight alone, and there is little prospect of a quick rapprochement between Syria and Iraq. In fact, the reduction of tensions in the region and the continued impotence of the PLO during 1982–87 is probably what eventually drove the Palestinians, in desperation, to seize the initiative.

Israel is now confronted with an internal, not an external problem. One and a half million Palestinians in Gaza and on the West Bank have made it abundantly clear that they no longer will suffer Israeli rule, whatever its material benefits. Forty-two years after the original United Nations plan to partition Palestine, this idea finally is gaining acceptance among a growing number of Palestinians, offering a glimmer of hope for a political settlement between Israeli Jews and Palestinian Arabs.

The *intifada* has challenged Israel's moral fiber more than its security. To paraphrase the biting comment of the late, beloved Ernst Simon, the Palestine problem has become an internal Jewish concern in much the same manner that anti-Semitism is essentially an internal Christian problem.

However, a willingness to trade land for peace is anathema to the romantic messianists of Israel's nationalist camp. The stunning victory of 1967 blunted the pragmatic spirit which built Israel, and unleashed a fervor of religious-political triumphalism which transvalued Judaism itself. Settling Judea and Samaria, and even Gaza, suddenly loomed as the supreme commandment. Joshua superseded Moses, and his book of conquests that of the Torah. The Arab became Amalek reincarnate, and the "stranger" of the Bible, toward whom the Jew was commanded to feel empathy and show compassion, was redefined as a convert to Judaism. Menahem Begin added the bitter resentment still seething from the trauma of the Holocaust, which was now touted as a world-view and a basis for foreign policy. As the popular song of the seventies put it, *ha-olam kulo negdeinu,* "the whole world is against us."

The consequences of this mindset have been catastrophic: a misguided venture into Lebanon, a government held hostage by West Bank extremists, the privatization of arms, the brutalization of Israel's youth, and a refusal to address the Palestinian problem.

In his 1971 essay "Education for Humanity in Time of War," Yigal Allon observed: "If we will be a light unto ourselves, perhaps we will be a light unto others. Certainly not before." The Judaism of Gush Emunim is without light. The basest form of modern nationalsim in Jewish garb, it violates the most fundamental biblical injunction: "You shall not copy the practices of the land of Egypt where you dwelt, or of the land of Canaan to which I am taking you; nor shall you follow their customs" (Leviticus 18:3).

The Judaism I know cares deeply for the welfare of mankind. The Book of Genesis is not only about the promise of the land but also about its purpose. Abraham and his descendants were called by God to be a source of universal blessing, a model of virtue to counter the lure of paganism. The land was to be a laboratory for the formation of a righteous and just society. But the vision had first to be limned in suffering which would intensify the passion for justice. After his victory over the four kings, Abraham the warrior could have seized the land immediately. But the experience of oppression and slavery preceded the achievement of statehood. The Bible's ubiquitous compassion for the stranger, the non-Israelite, is rooted in the degradation of Egyptian bondage.

The land never was granted unconditionally. Its retention was regarded as deriving from the piety and justice of its body politic. To pervert God's law was to defile the land, which would lead to expulsion. As the Bible's visceral language commanded, "So let not the land spew you out for defiling it, as it spewed out the nation that came before you" (Leviticus 18:28).

God's impatience with Israel throughout the Bible is a measure of the universal stakes involved in His "choosing" of them. Mankind needs a mentor. After the flood failed to alter human nature, God decided to instruct humanity through the example of one people. Israel's waywardness imperils the very survival of the human race.

The Jews' long exilic ordeal deepened the message of Judaism's mission. Outside their homeland they again became the proverbial "stranger" of the biblical text. How they were treated would reflect the humanity of the nation in which they lived. The Jews' recurring struggle to maintain their distinctive faith and communal autonomy constituted an implicit claim for the inalienable right to be different. From the Roman Empire to interwar Europe, Jews sought legal protection for their religious and cultural independence. Their endurance and their success legitimized the value of religious and ethnic diversity. In the picturesque words of Moses Mendelssohn to Christian Europe: "Dear brothers, you are well-meaning. But do not let yourselves be deceived! To belong to this omnipresent shepherd, it is not necessary for the entire flock to graze on one pasture or to enter and leave the master's house through just one door."

Zionism did not triumph by betraying that noble legacy. The restoration of Zion would create, as Allon put it, "a model of a totally moral Jewish existence in a model human society." Judaism's particularism always had at its core an ecumenical thrust. Our exercise of power must continue to accord with the lofty moral standards we espoused when powerless, for the ultimate biblical sanction of a Jewish state is to validate our vision in the crucible of reality.

Conservative Judaism and Zionism: Towards the Twenty-First Century

LEE I. LEVINE

In 1988, a century after their emergence and forty years after their having achieved stunning successes, Conservative Judaism and Zionism have much in common; each also has much to contribute to the other as they grapple for new self-definitions.

The ideas informing much of Conservative Judaism and Zionism began crystallizing in mid-nineteenth-century Europe and America. Conservative Judaism looks back to Zacharias Frankel in Germany and Isaac Leeser in America, while early Zionism points to such European forerunners as Zvi Kalischer, Yehuda Alkalay, and Moses Hess. Each developed institutionally in the 1880s and 1890s.

Both movements achieved their declared goals in the aftermath of the Second World War, when the State of Israel was established and the Conservative Movement became the dominant form of American Judaism. Finally, today, both movements suffer from a certain malaise, and are engaged in a search for redefinition given new political, cultural, and religious realities.

For Zionism, the basic issue is no longer creating a political entity, but defining its political, social, and moral values, its Jewish dimension, and its relationships with Diaspora Jewry, its Arab minority, and neighboring Arab countries, as well as resolving the Palestinian question.

Conservative Jews, confronted with declining numbers and the apparent vitality of both the Orthodox and Reform movements, are confronted with these questions: how can the movement regain the élan and dynamism it had a generation ago—what is required ideologically, halakhically, and institutionally? How should rabbinic and lay leadership be developed to meet new challenges? How can our different institutions work together coherently and constructively? Do we have the strength and resolve to address these issues honestly and directly, and do we have the tenacity to see our solutions through to completion?

The similarities between Conservative Judaism and Zionism are expressed in the core of their respective ideologies.

1. Both movements are historically oriented. It is history that brought the *halutzim* (pioneers) back to Israel, served as the bedrock for all Zionist ideologues, and provided the rationale for recognition of the Jewish homeland and the Jewish state, from the Balfour Declaration to Israel's Declaration of Independence.

Likewise, the Conservative Movement is firmly rooted, academically and halakhically, in an historical view of Judaism. As midrash served our ancestors in antiquity, and philosophy in the Middle Ages, so history has become the handmaiden of all Jewish reserach. The slogans that capture the essence of the Conservative halakhic approach all pertain to historical dimension, i.e., "tradition and change," "normative development," and "dynamic halakhah."

2. Given its historical orientation, each movement has developed a special affinity for the ancient period, which is viewed as representing its roots and antecedents. For Zionism, the First and Second Temple periods provide a touchstone for the modern nationalist experience. For its part, Conservative Judaism focuses on the rabbinic period, which is viewed as the greatest era of literary and spiritual creativity in postbiblical Judaism, and which produced what we now think of as "normative Judaism."

3. Conservative Judaism and Zionism also share a desire to recreate the fullest possible expression of Jewish life. Kaplan's concept of Judaism as a civilization, the synagogue-center as the movement's primary institutional expression, and the success of Camp Ramah in creating a total Jewish experience in Jewish space for an extended period of time all attest to Conservative Judaism's

integrative and inclusive scope. For its part, the State of Israel represents the totality of Jewish living in such areas as having majority status, language, the yearly calendar, control of media and governmental institutions.

4. Conservative Judaism and Zionism both attempt to create viable centrist alternatives to other ideologies. Conservative Judaism's centrist position between Orthodoxy and Reform on the American-Jewish scene is long-standing. In the nineteenth century, Zionism posed an alternative between the ghetto and medieval corporate framework on the one hand, and assimilation (e.g., living as "Germans of the Mosaic persuasion") on the other. In the late twentieth century, Israeli society finds itself being pulled both "backwards" to medieval ultra-Orthodox obscurantism and "forwards" to Gush Emunim messianism. Israeli society also is caught between a highly charged nationalism (of both a religious and a secular variety), where the verse *am levadad yishkon* ("a people that dwells alone") holds sway, and Westernization in language, habit, style, and taste, so that the phrase *am ke-khol ha-amim* ("a nation like any other nation") becomes more apt.

In response to extremism, Zionism and Conservative Judaism stand for intelligent moderation. In a deeper sense, both Conservative Judaism and Zionism walk the fine line between particularism and universalism, between the Jewish tradition and modernity. These ostensibly contradictory perspectives can exist harmoniously as long as they remain theoretical, like two books containing opposite viewpoints on the same shelf. Once these perspectives are put into practice, however, the results often are wrenching.

Given these similarities, Conservative Judaism and Zionism each can offer the other an opportunity or a setting it needs.

First, what Conservative Judaism can offer Zionism: clearly the major challenge facing Israeli society today is internal. The military and political challenges contronting Israel are secondary to the threats to Israeli Jewry's social and cultural cohesion. Tragically, the Jewish tradition, which might lend unity to Israeli society, is instead itself a source of strains, for the chasm between much of Israeli Jewry and the Jewish tradition has widened considerably during the past two decades. The emergence of a messianic nationalism, along with the growing power of anti-Zionist, ultra-Orthodox elements and the racist platform of a Rabbi Kahane (all speaking in the name of religion) project Judaism as anti-democratic and intolerant. These groups not only oppose, they attempt to delegitimatize Arab rights, the Jewish status of Ethiopian immigrants, Masorti and Reform rabbis, and all non-Orthodox religious services. In Me'ah She'arim and elsewhere, even the legitimacy of the State of Israel is questioned!

What is at stake today in Israel is nothing less than the Jewishness of the Jewish state. The Israeli religious establishment has succeeded in alienating much of the public from any kind of meaningful association with the Jewish tradition, Jewish peoplehood, and the Diaspora.

This is the challenge that the Masorti Movement is attempting to address. On one level, the movement is about the development of synagogues, a network of schools (Tali), a youth movement and camps, adult education activities, a kibbutz and moshav, and a newly founded Bet Midrash. On a deeper level, however, Masorti is the saga of a small but growing cadre of Conservative olim and sabras attempting to create a new option for a religiously polarized country: a vision of society which is both Jewish and pluralistic, committed and tolerant, nationalist and morally sensitive.

Our goal is to create a strong religious center to stabilize the society, a position that is not merely a compromise between extremes but that synthesizes the best of existing alternatives into more meaningful models. This Conservative/Masorti approach is being applied to Torah study, halakhic interpretation, morally informed social and political proposals, and institution building.

Just as the Conservative Movement addresses moral issues in contemporary American society from a halakhic perspective, so must the Masorti Movement breach the barriers that largely limit halakhic activity in Israel to the realm of ritual. As Abraham Joshua Heschel so aptly remarked, "There must be *mashgehim* [certifiers of kashrut] in banks and not only in butcher shops." The silence of the Orthodox establishment on broader social issues is as deafening as it is unforgivable.

Only the Conservative Movement, with the flexibility inherent in its appraoch to halakhah, can deal with a key issue ignored to date by halakhists: the bestowal of a special halakhic status on the

State of Israel, which would endow it with a legitimate, recognized standing within Jewish tradition. Finally, the Conservative Movement is in a unique position to bring both Judaism and Zionism into a healthy and constructive relationship with the best of modern culture. By so doing, it can fashion a comprehensive vision of the Jewish state which will be compelling for Jews in the twenty-first century.

The influence of Conservative Judaism in Israel would be greatly enhanced were fifty thousand or one hundred thousand Conservative Jews to make aliyah. Such a development would catapult the Masorti Movement to center-stage on the Israeli scene, and would redound to the benefit of the Conservative Movement worldwide. Unless large-scale Conservative aliyah occurs, however, the building of Masorti institutions in Israel will be a slower, far more deliberate process.

What can Zionism contribute to Conservative Judaism?

Israel offers an arena for the ultimate legitimization of the Conservative approach to Judaism. It challenges Conservative Judaism to transcend its American setting and become a world movement.

Today, American Jewry may be the largest Jewish community, but it is still a minority within world Jewry (six million out of some fourteen million people). The ratio between American and Israeli Jewry is rapidly changing. In 1914, there were forty Jews in the United States for every one in Israel. By 1948, that ratio shrank to 10:1; by 1975, to 2:1; today, it is about 1.6:1. Median projections by demographers indicate that sometime around 2010, Israel will become the largest Jewish community in the world. The growth rate of Israeli Jewry, and the decline in American Jewry, will contribute to this change. (Today, although the Jewish population of Israel constitutes about twenty-five percent of the world Jewish population, over forty percent of all Jewish babies are born in Israel). When Israel surpasses American Jewry demographically, the latter may well lose its special status on the world Jewish scene.

In addition, the Jewish people has begun to focus its power in international institutions connected in a variety of ways to the State of Israel. These include the Jewish Agency, the World Zionist

Organization, Keren Hayesod, the United Jewish Appeal, the Joint Distribution Committee, and the Council of Jewish Federations, as well as Jewish multinational organizations, such as the World Jewish Congress. It has been estimated that the Jewish people, including the State of Israel, spends $36 billion a year on public services, ninety percent of which passes through this network of organizations. Thus, the Conservative Movement must build ongoing ties to this network, rather than only approaching it annually to demand a fair share of its budget.

In the past, the Conservative Movement has been plagued by parochialism. During the 1950s, 1960s, and 1970s, the involvement of the movement nationally, and of local rabbis and lay leaders, in the emerging Federation-UJA world was minimal. While many individual Conservative Jews supported the Zionist movement in the past, our leadership in the United States was so focused on institution-building that it often seemed to ignore the Zionist enterprise. We cannot allow this narrow focus to continue today, as the "action" on the world Jewish scene focuses ever more heavily on Israel.

If we hope to broaden our movement internationally and appeal to the almost four and one-half million Diaspora Jews outside the United States, then Israel, and not America, must be our base. Few world Jewish communities are looking for an American religious import. Their societies and cultures are different from America's; Jewishly, they often are much more tradition-bound. Conservative Jewry will most effectively reach these people via Jerusalem, not New York or Los Angeles.

To date, we do not have a world movement in any real sense. In a world which is constantly shrinking, this absence becomes a critical detriment to our ability to compete with other types of Judaism.

The American-centered ideology of our movement has done us a great disservice. The downplaying of the centrality of Israel in Conservative publications—from the Rabbinical Assembly Haggadah to the *Sim Shalom* Siddur to *Emet ve-Emunah*—undermines our credibility among world Jewry. Ideas such as "several foci of Jewish life," "Babylonia and Jerusalem," "the complementary roles of Eretz Israel and Diaspora" may be facts of life, given contemporary Jewish history. However, they are not authentic in terms of the Jewish tradition, which unequivocally posits the centrality of Eretz Yisrael.

One should not elevate fortuitous historical circumstances to the level of ideological necessity or desirability. In terms of Judaism and Jewish history, Los Angeles is not the promised land, Philadelphia, Chicago, or Miami cannot substitute for Zion, nor can New York ever replace Jerusalem as the center of Jewish interest and yearning. To argue otherwise is to deny a major component of our religious and national heritage. For our literature, holidays, mitzvot, history, holy sites, and future dreams are inextricably intertwined with Eretz Yisrael.

The above is not intended to minimize the other challenges facing the Conservative Movement in America. I suggest, however, that the challenge and opportunity posed by Zionism and the State of Israel ought to be the first, not merely another, item on the movement's agenda. Only bold ventures in Israel, coordinated by *all* branches of the Conservative Movement, can galvanize us to make a significant and sustained contribution to the evolution of Judaism. An Israel-focused Conservative Movement also will make other tasks of the movement easier to accomplish.

Ultimately, the historical vindication of Conservative Judaism—beyond America and beyond the twentieth century—is only attainable through our success in Israel. Only thus will we be regarded as a major force shaping Jewish history in the twentieth and twenty-first centuries, not as a passing phenomenon.

Fortunately, there already has been an enormous change of attitude toward Israel by the Seminary, and the movement at large, during the past two decades. A decade ago, the reaction to some emerging Masorti institutions often was ambivalent; today there is widespread support and enthusiasm. Six years ago, the Seminary began promoting Conservative Judaism in Israel by actively assisting in the founding of an Israel-based rabbinical seminary, as well as establishing a support organization, the Foundation for Masorti Judaism, for the fledgling sister movement in Israel. Today, the Seminary's leadership is planning imaginative new ventures which will deepen this involvement. A new post–World War II generation is at the helm of the movement today. The product of the "flowering" of Conservative Judaism, it offers a new spirit and will promote opportunities and modes for Jewish expression.

We are committed to two of the most important enterprises in modern Jewish history, Conservative Judaism and Zionism, which should not be viewed as separate but equal. They can and must be linked. For Zionism desperately needs the most enlightened of Western values, culture, and Jewish religious expression, as embodied in the best of Conservative Judaism. The Conservative Movement in turn needs Zionism as an ideological focal point to lend it a renewed sense of purpose and as an avenue to affect contemporary and future Jewish life.

Do we care enough about Conservative Judaism and Zionism to link them firmly? The answer is not "in the heavens above, nor beyond the horizons"; it is here, in our hearts, our minds, our grasp.

SEMINAR 1
Democratic Values in the State of Israel

Where should our movement stand on such issues as the gap between rich and poor in Israel, civil liberties, the adoption of a constitution, protection for the rights of non-Jewish minority groups in Israel, how to respond to extremes of the right and left, and related issues? How do we balance the demand of Enlightenment conceptions of the state against those flowing from the special circumstances presented by the Jewish State of Israel?

Participants in this session were asked to keep in mind that another seminar would focus on religion in Israel and yet another would be devoted to the issues of peace, land, and security. Thus, Seminar 1 would try to focus upon the quality of democracy within the Green Line, excluding to whatever extent possible, issues of religion and state. Obviously, events in the territories and religious policies bear upon the central concern of this seminar, but we did not want to urge emphasis on the areas noted above.

Conservative Judaism's Role in Fostering Democratic Values

SHOSHANA S. CARDIN

I am a Conservative Jew who believes that we are a spiritual people, with particularist religious traditions, as well as a nation with a common heritage, culture, memory, and destiny. I do not subscribe to the belief that Judaism and democracy are antithetical, but rather that our challenge is to help fashion a democracy unique to Judaism. By this I mean a sovereign state that reinforces Jewishness, that respects Shabbat, that encourages me to express and develop my Jewish spirituality. I also believe that those who hold different views or beliefs should exercise their preferences, but without negating mine.

As I was taught during childhood, the Zionist dream and ideal is for us to have our own sovereign Jewish State in Eretz Yisrael, where we can become one people, with one language and one culture. There, we will constitute a national majority, responsible for our own destiny. The raison d'etre for this goal was articulated initially by Leo Pinsker in *Auto-emancipation:* "We are everywhere guests and nowhere the host." If we had our own sovereign state, we, the Jewish people, would be recognized as a nation among other nations; never again would we be stateless and powerless.

Coming from a secular Zionist home, I accepted the concepts of *halutziut* ("pioneering"), the purchase of land in Eretz Yisrael, and what became known as "productivization," the pragmatic socialist approach to achieving the ideal of nationhood. Further, this sovereign state, as envisioned by Aḥad Ha-Am, would become the creative center of the Jewish world. Thus, the "Judenstaat" (Jewish state), as envisioned by Herzl and others, would be both a political achievement and a social model.

The nature of this nation-state rarely was questioned. Clearly, it would be democratic and a living manifestation of our ethical teachings. It would be founded on the moral percepts of our prophets and sages: truth, justice, and the sanctity of human life, based on the belief that each human is created in the image of God. Some even believed that the Jewish State would become *or legoyim,* "a light unto nations."

In the euphoria of the U.N.'s partition vote in 1947, and given the desperate need for a refuge after the Holocaust as well as Israel's immediate rejection by the Arab world, questions on how such a vision was to be achieved went largely unanswered.

Any doubts about the democratic tenor of the new state were allayed by the memorable wording of its Delcaration of Independence, May 14, 1948:

> The State of Israel . . . will be based on freedom, justice and peace as envisaged by the prophets of Israel; it will ensure complete equality of social and political rights to all its inhabitants irrespective of religion, race or sex; it will guarantee freedom of religious conscience, language, education and culture.

A constitution was to follow later that year, but the continuing security crises precluded the necessary deliberations. In 1988, a draft constitution was circulated for study and comment, with the anticipation of a referendum on its adoption.

I served as an elected delegate to the 1967 Maryland constitutional convention, where we wrote the model state constitition for the twentieth century—only to have it thoroughly defeated in a referendum. In the intervening years, most of the concepts and proposals have been implemented through legislation or administrative initiative. From this experience, I learned that too much specificity and too many challenging concepts in a constitution can be counterproductive.

We have an obligation to become familiar with the draft Israeli constitution, to offer comment and criticism. We should support those who are promoting adoption of a constitution as a further clarification and safeguard of the democratic reality of Medinat Yisrael (the State of Israel).

I acknowledge being ambivalent about the ramifications for the Jewishness of a democratic Jewish state. The proposed constitution states, under the provision *freedom of religion and conscience,* Section 22, (d) 5: "Nothing in this section shall . . . affect any provisions pertaining to ritual fitness (*kashrut*) of food in the Israel Defence Force or in public institutions." I fully approve of this provision, though some may think it an infringement of personal rights or individual prerogative, for I want Israel to be Israel, not a United States for Jews. In addition, I approve of the inclusion of Hebrew as the official language, with special status for Arabic.

I appreciate the draft constitution's explicit references and assurances that the State of Israel will be a democratic state, and that every Jew has the right to immigrate and acquire Israeli nationality. The constitution appears to ensure a democratic state of and for Jews, but not necessarily a "Jewish state."

As an American, I live with the tensions between religion and state, individualism and obligation, universalist democratic principles and particularist Jewish tenets. Should we "answer to a higher authority" in the constitution of Medinat Yisrael? The current version has no reference to either God or Judaism.

As to the question whether non-Israeli Jews have the "right" to criticize Israeli actions, if we are one people, if we share a common heritage and destiny, then we must speak up and express that mutuality of responsibility.

I do not accept the view that my Jewishness or Zionism is diminished because I live in the United States. I may live in the Diaspora, but I am not in Galut (exile). I firmly believe that my future as an American Jew is inextricably tied to the future of the State of Israel, both its physical survival and its cultural-spiritual flourishing.

We should help educate Israelis that we are valid cultural and ideological partners. Generally, we will not be making aliyah, but we can, and wish to, be much more than fair-weather relatives. We understand democratic principles, the tensions and checks and balances which are necessary for effective governance. We should be called upon for counsel in matters of civil and human rights, and we are ready to speak out and support, in Israel, those actions which uphold and promote ethical values. We reserve the right to question actions which confuse or disturb us, mindful that making ultimate decisions regarding state security is not our domain.

When we look at the diversity of cultures, both Jewish and non-Jewish, and the growing divisiveness and hostility among them, we should turn to Isaiah's instruction to "learn to do good, seek justice, relieve the oppressed, defend the fatherless, plead for the widow" (1:17).

In Leviticus 19:34 we learn: "but the stranger that dwelleth with you shall be unto you as one born among you, and thou shall love him as thyself; for you were strangers in the land of Egypt." If that is the attitude mandated toward the "stranger," how much more is due the citizen, though he or she be non-Jewish?

But where do realpolitik and idealism meet? How can we, a continent and an ocean away, satisfy our strong desire as a people to behave in a moral and just fashion, while avoiding actions that jeopardize Israel's fragile security? We must remember that Israel is still a nation at war, and that preservation of human rights cannot become a prescription for suicide.

Most Israelis are unfamiliar with the tenets of democracy, not having been taught democratic principles of statehood. We must ally with those Israelis who share our vision of a democratic Jewish state. The Conservative leadership in Israel can play a very special role, both in the Tali schools and in informal settings, in helping educate Israelis on the moral imperatives both intra-Jewish and Jewish-Gentile, stemming from democratic principles.

We should help Israelis understand the tensions inherent in a commitment to pluralism and diversity. The attempt to homogenize many ethnic groups into one culture often can stir resentment and divisiveness. We have witnessed this with both the Sephardic communities and Ethiopian Jews in Israel, as well as with America's ineffective, frustrating, and potentially destructive "melting pot" theory.

Israel has had a coalition government since its inception. The current reality is that a very small party with a handful of seats can wield immense power by aligning with one major party, often exacting an exorbitant political "fee." In addition, under the present system, voters cast their ballots for political parties, not individuals. Each party submits a list with candidates ranked in numerical order. This system discourages individuals with talent and ability from important leadership positions; it also frustrates voters who cannot influence the system. Israel could benefit from, and Conservative Jews should endorse, an electoral system which would enable a majority party to win without concessions to a minority party.

America's Conservative leadership should educate their constituents on the daily realities of Israeli life. More American Jews must realize that Israel is not America in "Jewish miniature," nor is that our goal. We are two distinct democratic societies, fashioned by different political forces. Israel's cultural, economic, and geopolitical circumstances preclude any sudden, monumental changes, which will require education, exposure, and involvement.

American Jews and Israelis alike need to know that democratic values and principles did not spring *de novo* from the Anglo-American tradition, but are rooted in Jewish teachings. It was our ethos that promulgated respect for the dignity of each individual.

We must speak out against those voices which jeopardize that ideal. Ben-Gurion said, "Our ideals are the most realistic thing in our lives." We cannot permit fanaticism and demagoguery to prevail.

We should promote a multitude of successful social, educational, and cultural programs in Israel, rather than think of Israel as defined only by the beneficiaries of the Jewish Agency. There is a larger, highly complex society with which we must develop opportunities for interaction. We need meaningful exchanges, not limited to Conservative or other American *olim* (immigrants), with Israelis who are concerned about the democratic nature of Israel. As Israeli Supreme Court Justice Aharon Barak recently stated, "Democracy does not defend itself, it cannot fight for itself, you have to fight for it."

We Conservative Jews also should help young Israelis better understand the positive role Jewish spirituality and practice can play in life. Secular Israelis in particular need models of religious behavior, and a commitment to the whole Jewish people (not only in Israel) if we are to retain the spiritual component of our peoplehood.

In this, Israel's fortieth year of remarkable accomplishments and terrible anguish, we would do well to recall the insights of David Ben-Gurion:

> The Jews of Israel will never be able to compete in physical power with neighbors who do not accept their right to exist. But for thousands of years, the Jews have survived because of their moral qualities. While populating the land and making it fruitful, while creating economic and cultural enterprises, they will survive only if they maintain their moral, spiritual and intellectual standards. These have been the secret of their existence for four thousand years.

It is our obligation as Zionists to assist in the maintenance of these "moral, spiritual and intellectual standards" here and in Israel, particularly at a time of unprecedented moral dilemmas and intra-Jewish polarization, realizing that the dream of a Jewish state was a world Jewish enterprise. Our determination to be "a light unto nations," an exemplar of democratic values and justice, must be the same. We, Conservative Jewry, must participate in supporting democracy in Israel with a full heart, for it not we, who?

SYNOPSIS OF PROPOSED ACTIONS

1. Clearly articulate, in Israel as well as in the United States, that Conservative Jewry is committed to the welfare and continuity of the State of Israel.
2. Speak out and take positions in Israeli public media and journals so that the Conservative leadership plays a visible role in democratic endeavors as well as religious ones.
3. Study the proposed Israeli constitution so as to participate in informed dialogue on it. Offer political and financial assistance to those working for it.
4. Support electoral reform and offer personal and financial assistance on its behalf.

5. Join coalitions in Israel working to maintain a democratic Jewish state.
6. Develop programs to teach democratic principles in both formal and informal settings in Israel.
7. Develop U.S.–Israeli exchange programs to help dispel misunderstandings about the differences between our societies and political systems.
8. Promote discussions in synagogues and Conservative Jewry publications about our role in Israel and our vision of Zionism.
9. Promote in-depth visits, enabling Americans to develop personal relationships with Israeli peers.

A Conservative/Masorti Perspective

DAVID M. GORDIS

The November 1988 Israeli elections reaffirmed the reality of the Jewish people as a proactive presence in world events, and offered Israel a new opportunity for self-definition. The high level of participation in the election and the rejection of interference by outsiders attest to Israel's vibrant democracy, which represents the fulfillment of a fundamental Zionist goal.

The choices that were made, however, may prove disastrous for Israel, and, because of Israel's centrality in Jewish life, fateful for world Jewry. The election thus raises again the role of non-Israelis in the country's decision-making. During the campaign, the familiar refrain frequently was heard that Diaspora Jews had no business expressing views about candidates, parties, or issues: "If you want to participate, come and live here. Otherwise, remain silent. Our lives and those of our children, not yours or your children's, are on the line." Since the election, I've heard this repeated with a new twist. In apportioning partial blame for the recent "Who is a Jew?" eruption of Diaspora Jewry, we were told: "If you had come here in significant numbers, it would have been different."

Well, it might; I certainly wish to encourage aliyah by Jews committed to religious pluralism. Yet while the assertion that decisions about Israel's future must be made by her citizens alone is unassailable, it does not follow that we ought to remain silent. Israelis generally insist upon Israel's centrality in Jewish life, a plank in the Jersualem platform that defines Zionism. While accepting the principle, I maintain that centrality can be defined in many different ways; it need not imply the peripherality of all else in Jewish life. However defined, the principle necessarily implies the existence of a world Jewry beyond the center whose fate is intimately related to that of the State of Israel. It is inconsistent to accept the principle of Israel's centrality and to argue that non-Israelis are legitimate parties to deliberations regarding the State's character. I do not suggest that Israeli voting rights be extended to non-citizens of the state, only that an imposed silence, based on the argument that only Israelis "have a stake" in Israel's future, is unacceptable.

This observation particularly pertains to the Conservative Movement, which always has been committed to Zionism, and which, in the face of tremendous legal and political obstacles, has worked to develop its Israeli component, the Masorti Movement. Thus, the movement should engage, straightforwardly and energetically, issues relating to the character of the State of Israel. We should articulate and project an alternative liberal religious vision rooted in Jewish tradition and free of religious coercion. We should explore new modes of introducing Jewish religious values into Israel's public arena in the struggle to define the Jewishness of a free and democratic society. Our American experience, and our ideological and pragmatic focus, can make a real contribution to deliberations over the state's future. We also should support those Israelis who share our vision.

Our educational programs should convey a point of view about achieving the just society. World Jewry's role in general, and the Conservative Movement's in particular, should not be limited to discussions of Israel's strategic, political, and economic needs, for, more than ever, we should participate in deliberations on issues of social ethics and public policy.

The dramatic ascent of extreme Orthodox parties in Israel has caused non-Orthodox voices in Israel and the large majority of American Jews to express alarm with apparent unity. Yet the chasm separating Israelis from Diaspora Jewry is deep, as reflected in the recent debate over changing the Law of Return. By and large, the Law of Return is no issue for Israelis, except insofar as it might diminish American Jewry's financial and political support. For American Jews, democratic values in Israel are of little or no concern except as they affect their own status as Conservative or Reform Jews. The concern over extremist Orthodoxy, then, is radically different for the two communities. This is a result of Israeli unfamiliarity with Diaspora Jewish religious diversity (the product of the Orthodox monopoly over Israeli Jewish religious life) and of American Jewish unfamiliarity with threats to Israelis' democratic values. Overcoming this gap in understanding and knowledge is the principal challenge facing those concerned with the future of Israel-Diaspora relations.

The Masorti Movement in Israel should educate the Israeli public about Jewish religious diversity and should project an enlightened and progressive Jewish religious voice in shaping Israel's values. The Conservative Movement in America should educate its constituency concerning threats to Israeli democracy and develop partnerships with progressive forces in Israel so that Conservative Judaism's values can be brought to bear on Israeli society.

The case for democracy in Israel is not self-evident. Advocates of a fundamentalist, theocratic Israel do not believe that Israel should be a democratic state, that it should stand for equality of opportunity, equal standing before the law, or ethnic/religious pluralism. They reject totally the principle of separation of religion and government, often doing so cogently and consistently. Their understanding of the divine covenant with Israel, which informs their understanding of the nature of a Jewish state, should be responded to, not vilified. Their advocacy of expulsion of Arabs from Israel and the West Bank may be painful and repugnant, but it is "logical." They ground their positions in scriptural references, so that a debate based on an exchange of biblical or rabbinic sources will prove fruitless. Our role must be to offer, creatively, energetically, and persusasively, a vision of a different Judaism that is the basis for an exemplary society.

On the fateful issues of the Jewish character of Israel, the status of minorities in Israel, and the future of the West Bank and Gaza Strip, there are no perfect, or even good, options. The choices are between bad and worse. Given that the perpetuation of the status quo is itself a choice, we must assess alternatives, and select the "least bad" among them.

I propose we use three criteria—historical, moral/ideological, and pragmatic—in approaching the issue of democratic values in the State of Israel.

Historical. When the State of Israel was established, its Declaration of Independence declared it a democratic state. While it was to be a state for the Jewish people, its Jewish character was not to be achieved by discriminating against its non-Jewish residents by creating different classes of citizens. The state promised equality of standing before the law. There was to be no state religion. Israel's Jewish character was assured because more of its population, and its calendar, language, and daily rhythms, were Jewish.

In transforming the Jewish people's exilic past, Israel represented a kind of continuity with it as well. It viewed itself as linked with earlier periods of independent Jewish existence; it was transforming the nature of Jewish national life, not creating it *ex nihilo*. The developing Israeli culture would be predominantly Jewish, and would define Israel as a democratic Jewish state.

Israel should continue to institutionalize democratic values in law, public policy, and education. The burden of proof, in terms of historical arguments, is on those who seek to change the state's character, not on those who wish to maintain it.

Moral/ideological. There are those who, while acknowledging that Israel was established as a democratic state, argue on either religious or secular grounds that its character should now be altered. The religious argument refers to the covenantal relationship between God and the Jewish people, and points to the profanation of the Land through secularization and liberalization as the source of its internal and geopolitical problems. Its advocates note that God promised the Land of Israel to the Jewish people, on condition that it be "purified" of any alien (non-Orthodox or Gentile) presence. Such cleansing will prepare the way for the Messiah, whose coming is now, for the first time since the destruction of the Second Temple, within the Jewish people's grasp. Under this cosmology, considerations of human rights, equal protection under law, and democratic values are viewed as anachronistic. Proponents of this argument seek the establishment of God's rule in the land of Israel. Divine rule is not democratic; it is the ultimate authoritarian political philosophy.

The secular version of this argument is millenarian rather than messianic. It looks towards a golden age of Jewish restoration rather than the coming of the Messiah to establish God's kingdom. All Jewish history must culminate in the establishment of a pure Jewish existence in an independent Jewish state. This is seen as the "normalization" to which Zionism aspires, an end to Jewish marginality and intergroup relationships, a pure and homogeneous Jewish existence.

The shaping of this Jewish polity must be achieved by Jews, not by "Jews and others." Granting non-Jews who live in Israel equal rights and equal participation contravenes the historical process in which the Jewish people are engaged. Consequently, "strangers" should neither be integrated in Israeli society nor granted equality of status. Rather, their departure should be encouraged. As long as they remain, they should do so fully recognizing that their participation in shaping Israeli society will be severely circumscribed.

Opponents of an egalitarian and democratic Israel cannot be refuted logically, for they simply view God and the world differently from proponents of democratic values in Israel. The only possible response to their arguments is to project alternative visions of Jewish history, the role of the State of Israel, and the meaning of the divine covenant as it related to the land.

The Conservative movement's value system derives both from Jewish tradition as we understand it and from our critical reading of the Western humanistic tradition. Our tradition is replete with expressions of humanistic concerns. Fundamental to our stance toward non-Jews is the biblical imperative of compassion and sensitivity towards the "stranger."

> You shall have one law, for the citizen and for the stranger who dwells in your midst.
>
> (Exodus 12:49)
>
> Do not oppress or persecute the stranger, for you were strangers in the land of Egypt.
>
> (Exodus 22:20)
>
> You know the soul of the stranger, because you were strangers in the Land of Egypt.
>
> (Exodus 23:9)

It is an everlasting law that the stranger is to be like you before the Lord. You are to have one law and one justice, for you and for the stranger who lives with you.

(Numbers 15:15–16)

The respect for each human life is expressed in Scripture and in such rabbinic literature as "he who destroys a single human being, it is as if he destroyed an entire world" (Mishnah Sanhedrin 4:5). (The context establishes with certainty that this statement pertains to non-Jews as well as Jews.) Before God, all people are equal, Jew and Gentile alike.

This theme of universal concern and equality coexists with more particularistic and ethnocentric sources. It is here that the Conservative Movement's belief that not all sources are equally authoritative must be articulated. Most of us reject basing maximalist territorialist demands on biblical promises. We are aware that adherents of other traditions, on the basis of their sacred texts, come to different conclusions than those reached by Jewish literalists. The evolving perception of the Jewish people, refined and sharpened both by historical experience and interaction with the Western humanistic and other influences, must select some aspects of the Jewish tradition as authoritative, while viewing others as obsolete.

While there is room for messianic aspiration in Conservative ideology, it cannot supplant our vision of the relationship between the Jewish people and others or rationalize a betrayal of basic Jewish/human codes of behavior. We should not hasten the Messiah's coming by repudiating the very content of the Messianic vision. That vision looks to Jewish national restoration in the context of mutually respectful relationships among peoples, a sensitivity to the innate dignity of all, and the rejection of the domination of any one group. The universal acceptance of the dominion of heaven will transcend any human sovereignty. This vision should be central in considering political and economic equality, the distribution of limited resources for social services, and the teaching of civic values in Israeli schools.

A political system must be able to sustain the social fabric by maintaining a network of relations among the society's disparate groups. It must also earn respect and support from countries whose support is vital.

Some argue that exchanging territory for peace and granting full equality to Israeli Arabs is unacceptable on security grounds and given the need to preserve the Jewish character of the state. But it is questionable whether a state can be secure and stable if it dominates a population which may become a majority and which rejects the state's sovereignty. The choice between a larger state controlling a hostile and rejectionist population and a smaller state enjoying domestic tranquility will be decided by Israel's citizens. What is beyond debate is the fact that the status quo will lead to disaster. The population time bomb is a reality. Expulsion of the Arabs of Israel and the territories is both morally outrageous and self-destructive, since it will bring the opprobrium of most of the world, including the United States. Israel must continue to rely on the United States, whose continued support very much would be at risk if "transfer" occurred. The perpetuation of a two-class structure in which Palestinian Arabs are without political rights perpetuates the frustration which fires the *intifada,* is perilous for Israel's international standing, and is morally offensive.

For historical, moral/ideological, and pragmatic reasons, then, the Conservative/Masorti Movement should promote an Israel which derives strength from its breadth of sympathy, capacity for empathy, and compassion with strangers who dwell in its midst. While the implications for our position on territorial compromise seem clear, our discourse should be as nonpolitical or, at least, nonpartisan as possible. Perhaps part of the Zionist achievement is that ideology and values deriving from the Jewish experience, as Jews of differing perspectives understand it, will again help shape political realities. Participating in formulating Jewish public policy is for us Conservative/Masorti Jews more than an option; it is a sacred obligation.

Zionism, Democracy, and Judaism

BARBARA SPECTRE

It is tempting to claim glibly that Judaism, democracy, and Zionism are not only compatible but mutually supportive. It would be a most gratifying assertion if it could be justified. My task, however, is to sharpen the discrepancies among these concepts so that the subject and its problematics can be discussed with integrity.

The concepts "democracy," "Zionism," and "Conservative Judaism" were not selected by chance as the subject of this seminar; they represent a convergence of motifs that have accompanied the Jewish people throughout their history. These three concepts reflect deeply rooted principles in the collective Jewish psyche. By examining the sources of these fundamentals, we might appreciate the tradition of conflict among them.

Genesis 12 represents the beginning of the Jewish people's history. Abraham is addressed by God: Go to a certain land, become a people, I am your God. The uniqueness of the bond among these three elements is expressed by Martin Buber in *On Zion: The History of an Idea*.

> It is impossible to imagine a historical Israel as existing at any time without belief in its God or previously to such belief: It is precisely the message of the common leader that unites the tribes into a people. It is no less impossible to imagine this belief as existing before and outside the land of Israel. It is an absolutely historical belief, the belief in a God leading the fathers, and then the whole people, into the promised land at historically determined times for divinely historical purposes.

Here is no "nation" as such and no "religion" as such but only a people interpreting its historical experiences as the actions of its God.

Buber's elucidation reveals why the terms "religion," "people," and "nation" are themselves distortions when applied exclusively to the Jewish manifold. Each was conceived not independently but in relation to the other two: their unity is the underlying reality.

The message in Genesis 12 is that there are not three elements, but really four; the fourth being the inextricable wedding of all three. This vision means that any of the three can betray the bond in one of two possible ways. The people can sin by rejecting God (e.g., the building of the golden calf) and/or by renouncing the land (e.g., the sin of the ten scouts). Similarly, the land can either deteriorate or flourish as a result of both relationships: when it is abandoned by the people and/or by God, it becomes desolate; when the people obey God, it flourishes. Even God and His Torah cannot be understood apart from the will of the people (*lo ba-shamayim hi*), nor can He be absent from the land without diminishing His Presence. Finally, the disruption of one of the bonds automatically affects the other, e.g., if the people sin against God, they are exiled from the land. The history of the Jewish people is replete with just these tensions.

The tensions are the result of inherent contradictions among the three elements. For example, between "God" and "people": adherence to the will of God both elicits and informs a theocentric perspective, in opposition to the concerns of a people, which by necessity encompass an anthropocentric posture. The intrinsic conflict is manifest in disputes over *Torah she-be-al peh* (the "oral Torah"). Is *Torah she-be-al peh* eternal (given on Mount Sinai), or do the concerns of a generation justify its emendation? Similarly, there are inherent tensions between "God" and "land": the spirituality of a religious world-view can well contradict the mundane realities of settling and governing a land (e.g., the Conquest). In general, how is the universalist mission of being *or la-goyim* ("a light unto the nations") to be reconciled with the particularism engendered by loyalty to a specific land? Finally, the tension inherent between "land" and "people" is reflected in the oft-mentioned conflict between the attitudes of Masada and Yavneh.

The three concepts of people, land, and God have found expression in modern ideologies. Democracy can be seen as the modern transposition of "the people." It is the belief that it is the just right of the people to establish and monitor their own modes of government; the will of the people has its own legitimacy. "The land" finds its modern ideological expression in Zionism: the belief in the Jewish people's right to sovereignty in their historic homeland. Lastly, the "ism" most appropriate to belief in God and His Torah is "Judaism," understood as adherence to the Jewish tradition as normative.

The various combinations of these three ideologies provide a schema for understanding the political map of Israel. Extremist parties espouse one of the principles, to the neglect or exclusion of the other two. Thus, the strict adherence to the need for a *Jewish homeland,* at the expense of ignoring democratic principles or precepts mandated by Judaism (such as how to treat the stranger), characterize the extreme nationalist parties, such as Kach. A second extremist pole, dedicated totally to *democratic* principles, denies the Jewish nature of the state, on the one hand, and the Zionist aspirations of the Jewish people (e.g., the Canaanite movement of the forties and fifties, and at present the ideology of the Israeli Communist Party). Sole and exclusive adherence to *Judaism* as the organizing principle, to the denial of Zionism or any democratic principles, defines a third extremist pole, that of the Neturei Karta. It must be emphasized that in and of themselves, each of the principles expressed by one of the extremist poles is laudable; what makes them objectionable is when they are adhered to in exclusion of the other two. Thankfully, each of these extremist groups is a minority.

The majority of political ideologies within the Jewish people today, however, can be seen as the possible combinations of two of the three guiding principles.

Thus, the espousal of Judaism and Zionist principles, often to the neglect of the democratic principle, is the foundation of the NRP (National Religious Party). Democratic dynamics are curtailed within this grouping because of the inherent contradictions alluded to above. The NRP's leaders might ask: How can the eternal precepts of Judaism be subject to the often uneducated and uncommitted will of the people? What will happen to the state's Jewish character if subject to public referendum? Public transportation, non-halakhic marriage, non-halakhic divorce all are issues which this party considers non-negotiable in the face of an apathetic and often antipathetic public.

A second major grouping is those parties who espouse both Zionism and democracy, but for whom the Jewish agenda is secondary. In these parties, the Jewish component is restricted, because of inherent contradictions between Judaism and democracy. The two major parties in Israel, which can be considered populist, are nourished ideologically from humanist, rationalist principles (Labor), or from deeply-rooted Jewish peoplehood experiences (Likud) that have elevated the people of Israel to a quasi-theological status. They differ mainly in the emphasis given the democratic and nationalist components of their platforms. Labor gives greater importance to democracy in the democratic/nationalist debate which is currently raging in Israel, while the Likud is a greater advocate of nationalist principles.

The largest grouping among the Jewish people promotes both the Judaic and peoplehood principles, but has not stressed the third, Zionist component; this in general defines Disapora Jewry. For some, aliyah is a matter of "not yet"; for others, remaining in the Diaspora results from contradictions between Jewish and Zionist principles. For example, some feel that Judaism has developed a universal agenda during its long history in the Diaspora which should not be negated by claiming that Judaism can only be realized in Zion. They feel that Judaism's universalist, spiritual dimension is contradicted by slavish adherence to particularist national aspirations; e.g., interrogation of Arabs for security reasons or the sale of arms to South Africa.

Two basic conclusions emerge:

1. While the vast majority of the Jewish people are organized around two of the three founding principles, no identifiable group is dedicated to the original vision: the ultimate synthesis of all three. But before we promote the amalgamation of all three principles as the desirable Masorati platform, we must acknowledge that there *are* deep-seated intrinsic incompatibilities among them. It is

for good reason that no other grouping, either political or ideological, has taken all three as its collective determination.[1]

2. The absence of the incorporation of all elements produces either extremism (parties devoted to one principle, to the exclusion of the other two), or, as with those ideologies dedicated to only two of the three principles, a world-view which cannot serve as the basis for the unity of the Jewish people, since one of the elements around which the Jewish people organize themselves is excluded.

Thus it seems that an ideology amalgamating the three principles would be highly desirable. But, given the inner contradictions, would not such an ideology be compromising our intellectual integrity? No, just the opposite. There is a dynamic operative between the three that makes the fusion both possible and necessary. Let us examine this dynamic by exploring more closely the conflicting aspects of "democracy" and "Judaism."[2]

The democratic principle is based upon the legitimacy of the people's will, which implies that decisions reached by the collective will have validity. By extension, this would seem to imply a belief in relativist truth. (One could avoid *total* relativism by saying that democracy does not necessarily claim that *what* the people decide is right; only that their decision-making is legitimate. In short, "the people have the right to make their own mistakes," as a popular aphorism has it.) Nevertheless, democracy does suggest that, at the least, humans can determine what is right. Scrutiny is an indispensable part of that determination, since people must judge what is correct. Most often, the right of scrutiny is instantiated in such institutions as the judiciary, where it functions as the right of appeal, and in the institution of a free press. Thus, democratic man, scrutinizing man, not only determines the norms of his society, but ultimately also the criteria by which to judge those norms. Because the criteria are not derived from any ultimate or authoritarian source, one can say that democratic premises are anthropocentrically based.

Further, democratic societies by nature tend to have relativistic world-views. For democracy to function properly, a majority must not coerce a minority; rather, the prevalent attitude should be that no one considers himself or herself in sole possession of the truth. Speaking about the requirements of liberal democracy, Justice

Oliver Wendell Holmes states: "Anyone who is free of doubt about the rightness of his opinion regards persecution of those holding other opinions as natural." The guarantee of the pluralistic nature of enlightened democratic societies is demonstrated in such measure as the separation of church and state, and the academic independence of institutions of higher learning. Formulations of democracy which do not allow for pluralistic opinions are hollow, if not dangerous.

The theocentric religious world-view stands in sharp contrast to the democratic one. It bespeaks of the eternal, not the contextual; of the absolute, not the relative. It promulgates a system of law which is not grounded in man's whims, considerations, and conveniences. For example, the Shabbat starts when Shabbat starts, and not when the observer gives his "O.K." Religious law offers man the opportunity to transcend the circularity of his own considerations. Anthropocentric man can scrutinize and legislate, but he cannot do the most important thing of all—lend his life significance. For the significance he seeks is to be part of something greater, but that is an honor he cannot confer upon himself. Man as the measure of all things cannot climb higher than his mortal "height"; in his most honest and darkest moments, he knows that.

Not only in the metaphysical realm does anthropocentric man experience dark moments. It is difficult, in the last decade of the twentieth century, to share unequivocally the beliefs that inspired the great democratic documents of the Age of Reason. We have assimilated into our consciousness not only the depth of the atrocities, but also the reality that the killers and spectators listened to Beethoven as the death trains passed by. What is anthropocentric man to do if even reason, which relies upon systematic doubt and scrutiny, must itself be doubted and scrutinized? A theocentric, absolute gounding for ethical judgments looks quite attractive in considering recent history.

What is interesting for our purposes is that the above paragraphs describe the theocentric Jewish perspective as a corrective for the democratic world-view. Absolute values serve as an antidote to the anarchistic possibilities of relativistic values. The reverse also is true. Rational questioning and skepticism serve as correctives to the excesses of fundamentalism, which an absolute system of truth can produce. Thus, the "contradiction" between the two systems may be productive.

This should not be surprising. Dialectic thinking is endemic to the Jewish religious tradition, whether to the Talmud's *shakla ve-tarya* (the give and take of talmudic discourse) or in the contradictions found in the oral Torah. Again, the three "contradictory" principles of God, people, and land, now converted into ideologies which divide as well as unite the Jewish people, may be necessary *correctives* to each other; perhaps they should be *institutionalized into a system of checks and balances*. An acknowledgment of the importance of this dynamic would mean that in Israel there must be a *mutuality* of correctives.

• Democratic methods should be fully embraced by the state, e.g., there should be a separation of synagogue and state. Democratic processes will serve a corrective to the fundamentalism to which Judaism, as much as any other religion, is susceptible. And, in any case, there will be a Jewish dimension to the Jewish state only because Jews want it that way. The more Judaism is legislated, the less they will want it. Israelis will eat matzot on Pesach not because the Knesset says so, but because the tradition is compelling to them. (It is, anyway, absurd to enforce a religious law on an unreceptive public, when a flight to Cyprus can circumvent any restrictions.)

Anyone who fears "Jewish anarchy" or the loss of the state's Jewish character demonstrates a weak belief in the power of Jewish ideas. Judaism will be enriched, not impoverished, by responding to the grief, the ennui, and the dilemmas of individualism to which modern Jews are susceptible.

Does this mean that Judaism is reduced to the anthropocentric criterion of "whether it suit us"? That travesty of the religious world-view might be the case if we did not allow that the corrective would provide balance in the other direction as well.

• Thus, mutually, the Jewish tradition can act as a corrective to the darker side of democracy. Only in a system informed by values and standards can Israeli Jews withstand the temptations of *yeridah* (emigration) and the superficial materialism to which an open society is susceptible. Thus, democracy in Zion must have a strong system of *Jewish* education.

Of course, Jewish education which acts as a corrective for the fallacies of democracy must also incorporate open questions and be based upon critical methodology. Otherwise, we have only substituted for the danger of openness the danger of indoctrination. Thus, the Tali school system is essential for a democratic Israel, and must be promoted until it is the rule rather than the exception.

• What is needed is a *formal mutuality of correctives*. Judaism can tolerate a complete separation of synagogue and state provided there is a strong system of Jewish education. Conversely, democracy can tolerate a Jewish education *provided* it is based upon the critical method, which, in a sense, is an intellectual counterpart to the right of appeal.

The Masorati Movement is the largest organized group of Jews in Israel which espouses the three principles of Zionism, democracy, and Judaism. Of necessity, therefore, its ideology will be conflicted and will not be easily communicated. But as long as the Masorati Movement maintains a vision which neglects none of the three, it will forge the Jewish, democratic nature of the State of Israel.

NOTES

1. The conflicting nature of these three fundamental elements also provides a schema for understanding Israeli current events. Thus, Israeli political issues can be viewed as (a) nationalist/religious conflicts (e.g., the exemption of a yeshiva boy from army service), (b) nationalist/democratic conflicts (e.g., the demographic problem of the territories), or (c) democratic/religious conflicts (e.g., religious legislation and coercion).

2. This paper did not address itself to the other two "dynamics of conflict": between Zionism and democracy, and Zionism and Judaism.

The Struggle for Democratic Values in the State of Israel

GAD UFAZ

INTRODUCTION

The State of Israel has been a democracy since its inception. It made the transition from an autonomous, democratic "settler society" to a sovereign, democratic nation-state. During the forty years of its existence, Israeli democracy became stronger both despite, and as a result of, the difficult trials and stark challenges with which it has contended. Only a few of the dozens of countries that have achieved independence in the past four decades can be classified as democratic. In most, the democratic tradition remains flimsy and fragile.

The achievement of a democratic society in Israel is among Zionism's most impressive achievements (among its others are the renaissance of nationhood revival of Hebrew as the language of daily life, and the absorption of several million immigrants from throughout the world). This achievement could not be taken for granted because the majority of olim (new immigrants), both prior to and since statehood, did not experience a democratic way of life prior to their aliyah. In addition, the Jewish people, whose religion is based on the precepts of halakhah (Jewish law), has not experienced political independence for two thousand years. Its conceptions of the structures of statehood were derived primarily from non-Jewish sources; "democracy" has no Hebrew equivalent to this day.

JUDAISM AND DEMOCRATIC VALUES

Given the rich diversity of classical Jewish sources, and the particular sophistication and openness of Midrash, one can find support for almost any point of view. Still, one can delineate a number of characteristic Jewish precepts which suggest considerable receptivity to democratic principles.

1. Israel's Declaration of Independence notes that the new state "will be . . . based on *freedom, justice* and *peace*, as envisaged by the prophets of Israel; it will ensure *complete equality* of social and political rights to all its inhabitants, irrespective of religion, race or sex . . ." (emphasis added).

This passage makes it clear that Israel's democratic philosophy is based upon the Scriptures. While the Greeks established the institutions of democratic government, the moral values that are its life-blood are derived primarily from the biblical view that all men are created in God's image (Genesis 1:26–27, 5:1, 9:6).

Rabbi Akiva said: "Beloved is man that he was created 'in God's image'; greater love was shown to him in that it was made known to him that he was created 'in God's image' " (Pirke Avot 3:14). Rabbi Akiva underscored the dignity inherent in each person when he elevated "thou shalt love thy neighbor as thyself" (Leviticus 19:18) as the central commandment of Judaism. Ben-Azzai maintained that the verse beginning "This is the book of the descendants of Adam" (Genesis 5:1) is an even greater principle, for it implies that all humans (not just Jews) descended from the first human, and thus share a basic worth and status.

Judaism teaches that all people are equal, yet each person is unique and special, for "the Supreme King of Kings, the Holy One, blessed be He, fashioned every man in the stamp of the first man, and yet not one of them resembles his fellow. Therefore, every single person is obliged to say: 'The world was created for my sake' " (Mishnah, Sanhedrin 4:5).

2. Judaism is committed to human freedom. Concerning the giving of the Ten Commandments at Mount Sinai, one key source underscores this commitment through a key wordplay: "And the tables were the work of God, and the writing was the writing of God, graven upon the tables (Exodus 32:16). Read not *ḥarut* [graven] but *ḥerut* [freedom]" (Pirke Avot 6:2).

The freedom, as opposed to enslavement to another human being, involves dedication to the infinite and eternal, the worship of God and study of Torah.

Thus, Rabban Yoḥanan ben Zakkai explained the ritual which signified the willing bondman (his ear was bored) in these terms: "Why was the ear singled out from all the other limbs of the body? The Holy One, blessed be He, said: This ear, which heard My voice on Mount Sinai when I proclaimed 'For unto me the children of Israel are servants . . .' (Leviticus 25:55), they are my servants, and not servants of servants, and yet this [man] went and acquired a master for himself—let it be bored!" (B.T., Kiddushin 22:2).

The Bible also expressed reservations about crowning a human king (Deuteronomy 17:14, I Samuel 8:10–22) rather than affirming God's reign. Gideon replied to those who asked him to rule over them: "I will not rule over you, neither shall my son rule over you; the Lord shall rule over you" (Judges 8:23). The Mekilta interprets the verse "And ye shall be unto me a kingdom of priests and a holy nation" (Exodus 19:6) as God saying, "I shall not appoint nor delegate anyone else, so to speak, to rule over you, but I myself will rule over you" (Mekilta Yitro 2).

Samuel finally acceded to the people's wishes and appointed a king over them "like all the nations" (I Samuel 8:22). In time, the monarchy was sanctified as an institution; it even became a symbol of the messianic age (the restoration of the House of David in "Greater Israel"). Yet Samuel, a political pragmatist, acted contrary to his religious convictions. If in a monarchy the national leader acted contrary to his religious principles to adhere to the popular will, all the more must he do so in a democracy, whose values are consistent with Judaism's spirit.

3. The Torah as a writ of covenant between the Jewish People and God is of central importance in the establishing of a democratic culture. The covenant is sustained by studying Torah and fulfilling the mitzvot agreed to by the entire nation: "We shall do and hear" (Exodus 27:7). The sages, steeped in Torah, are responsible for ensuring that the way of life it commands be kept. There are continual challenges to this elite group by other sages, so that its leadership continually rotates and no permanent leadership group can be formed.

The Torah portion *Nitzavim*, in which the covenant between God and the people is established, begins: "Ye stand this day all of you before the Lord your God; your captains of your tribes, your elders and your officers, with all the men of Israel" (Deuteronomy 29:9). Concerning this verse, the commentators have elaborated: "Though I have appointed for you captains, elders, and officers, you are all equal before me; as it is said, 'all men of Israel.' In other words, you are all responsible one for another" (Tanḥuma, Nitzavim 2 [my translation]).

This brief passage encompasses the world-view that has served as the cornerstone of Jewish communal life: mutual responsibility, tzedakah (charity), and halakhic decision-making by human consensus, not divine fiat. This kind of halakhic decision-making was reflected in the story of the disagreement between Rabbi Eliezer and Rabbi Yehoshua over the question of Akhnai's Oven (Bava Meẓia 59:2).

A *baraitha* (talmudic citation) attributed to Rabbi Yossi includes this description of democratic decision-making among the rabbis during the Second Temple period: "A halakhic question was posed. If they listened (agreed), they told them, and if not, they put the matter to a vote. If a majority found it profane, it was profane; if a majority found it pure, it was pure" (Tosefta, Ḥagigah 2:9 [my translation]).

Whether the Sanhedrin was an originally Jewish political institution or replicated a Greek model, this "supreme court" based its rulings on democratic, not "charismatic," procedures (e.g., a *bat kol,* or heavenly voice). In short, there are a complex of values in the Jewish tradition conducive to the acceptance of democratic rule. They include discouraging centralized leadership, recognizing the equal value of all men, and distributing among all the people responsibility for fulfilling the Covenant. The tradition believes in such open, enlightened values as protecting individual rights and minority interests. Small wonder, then, that the Jews have flocked to democratic countries in modern times, that they adapted so well to Western lifestyles, and that they created Israeli democracy.

True, halakhah easily can adapt itself to a secular, foreign culture, applying the rule: "The law of the state is law" (Bava Kamma 13:2). Yet this does not preclude the possibility of Israel being both an authentically Jewish and a democratic society. In fact, some of the state's political and sociocultural superstructure encourages the coexistence of halakhic and democratic values, e.g., religious kibbutzim. The general public, while generally nonobservant, exalts Jewish symbols and lives according to Jewish cultural norms.

THE PROSPECTS FOR ISRAELI DEMOCRACY

As a modern, secular movement of national liberation, Zionism always functioned in a democratic manner. Although Herzl was widely viewed as a messianic figurehead, he never adapted centralized leadership patterns. Herzl was a product of a humanistic, nationalist, Western culture. His followers, who generally had not experienced democracy in their countries of origin and were at times tempted to adopt more centrist policies, followed his democratic policies. The Zionist Congresses and the various Yishuv (prestate) institutions and organizations helped crystallize democratic norms of behavior, which ultimately determined the nature of the Israeli political system.

Democracy is a complex system of powers, checks, and balances adapted to the local culture. It functions despite the conflicting interests and internal contradictions of the diverse people it serves. Without such control mechanisms as freedom of information, equality under the law, personal freedoms, and majority rule tempered by a respect for minority rights, democracy has no chance of long-term survival.

Israel's young democracy, faced with threats from within and without, lacking tradition and hands-on experience, has withstood many dangers.

1. *Ethnic factionalization,* a focal issue as recently as the early 1980s, is now becoming increasingly marginal. Some oriental communities still tend to favor the nationalist, right-wing, and fundamentalist parties, and exhibit a propensity to forgo democratic principles, which they have not yet internalized. This phenomenon is reinforced by their lingering sense of social and economic insecurity, and by the ethnic stigmas to which they are sometimes subject.

2. *The existential insecurity prevalent in Israeli society.* The country's limited size and population, coupled with the persistent threat by larger neighbors, easily foster the longing for a strong authority figure who will provide the illusion of security.

3. *The weak position of the Knesset.* A fractionalized body, the Knesset has no real ruling majority with a clearly defined policy and program of action.

4. *The Jewish people's historical experience.* During centuries in the Diaspora, Jews both obeyed halakhah and often were alienated from local laws of the lands they inhabited. Viewing these laws as edicts designed to restrict, repress, and denigrate, they developed a tendency toward sophistry and evasion, so as to circumvent them. This disrespect for secular law has "carried over" among some of Israel's citizens.

5. *The rejection in principle of democratic values,* which has become entrenched in messianic, activist, religious circles, is the most blatant threat to Israeli democracy. Israel's religious messianists, while a relatively small group, comprise an elite imbued with a profound belief in the justice of its cause. It spawned the Jewish "underground," which gained the admiration of many who viewed it as the authentic heir to the pioneer settler tradition. Its highly educated, sophisticated members project via the mass media a sense of unassailable certainty that they are the true representatives of Jewish thought and tradition. Many Israelis accept this distortion because of their lack of familiarity with the sources.

Occasionally, in rare moments of candor, the adherents of antidemocratic thinking in Israel reveal their true face, as did Rabbanit Miriam Levinger several years ago: "Democracy has not proven itself sufficiently to warrant my support. Judaism has existed for 2000 years, and democracy is a fickle manipulation. In my opinion it is only a vessel, and certainly not a sacred value, just as Israeli law is not a sacred value. . . . Democracy is an alien value" (*Ha-Aretz,* Sept. 17, 1984).

As noted above, the view that Judaism and democracy are contradictory philosophies represents a distortion of the tradition. Still, adherents of anti-democratic thinking will take whatever action they deem necessary to achieve their goals.

SUMMARY

Discussion on how to foster greater democratic thinking and practice in Israel focuses primarily on such structural issues as the need for a formal constitution, instituting a constituency-based electoral system, and separation of church and state. Some advocate transition from a parliamentary to a presidential system of government, or the adoption of direct democracy (via plebiscites). Yet the problem of democracy may be more "cosmic," for the democratic tradition within the country is weak, and it is that, rather than particular structures, that needs strengthening.

Accordingly, the only guarantee for the quality and future of Israeli democracy is the educational system, which alone can ensure that future generations will support and strengthen democratic culture in Israel.

In the early years of statehood, a sense of ideological fervor, as well as a spirit of pioneering, democratic Zionist values, prevailed under the influence of fervent nationalism and external threats to Israel's existence. Today this solidarity has become eroded. The late Uriel Tal (in *Myth and Reason in Contemporary Judaism*, p. 135) captured what we have lost:

> The crisis which besets us . . . does not derive from the loss of faith . . . but from the loss of continuity. . . . We [in Israel] are in the midst of a process of exile—an exile from our sources, from the tradition. Zionism, as expressed in the return to Zion, has created a new exile—not an exile from the Land, but an exile from self-identity. From its inception, Zionism certainly never took into account that it was also possible to be alienated from Judaism in Hebrew.

Most Israelis are not only nonobservant, but also ignorant of Jewish sources, in part from the prevailing stigma associated in Israel with everything "religious" and from the Orthodox establishment's monopoly on all matters relating to "Judaism." Nationalist, messianic circles, led by Gush Emunim, strive to fill the growing spiritual void. These circles claim to be heirs to the tradition of pioneering, socialist Zionism. Many believe they are skillfully achieving their goals. For those bearing the banner of messianism, democracy is not a relevant value. They will not hesitate to take advantage of its weaknesses to replace it with a culture and a regime that are more "efficient" in achieving their goals.

The only way to overcome this threat to Israeli democracy is through education and through reconnecting contemporary Jews to traditional sources. This can be done through the creative use of classical midrash and the development of new midrashim which can appeal to Jews who are not "fearful of God."

TOPICS FOR DISCUSSION

1. The Conservative/Masorti Movement represents the integration of a halakhic lifestyle with modern, Jewish, democratic values. Therein lies its potential contribution to Israeli democracy.
2. The Conservative Movement can only express its full power and influence by allying with like-minded groups. It must exercise much sensitivity in seeking to solicit liberal allies in Israel and abroad to join in the struggle for an Israel that is both democratic and faithful to the Jewish tradition.
3. The Conservative Movement is strongest in the area of education. It should increase its allocation of resources for teaching Judaism and for developing modern commentary and midrash.
4. The Conservative Movement must also commit itself to a campaign of practical, political action in the Knesset and elsewhere in Israel's political system, in its legal system, and in the mass media.
5. Anything of significance that affects Israel will necessarily have repercussions for American Jewry, and vice versa. Therefore, the issue of fostering democratic values in Israel must involve American Jews, who should adopt specific positions and strategies to strengthen Israeli democracy, lest an irreparable schism develop between the two communities.

SELECTED BIBLIOGRAPHY

1. אונח מ', **הקהילה החדשה**, הקיבוץ המאוחד, תל־אביב, תשמ"ח.
2. אלון מ', **המשפט העברי**, מאגנס, ירושלים, תשל"ג.
3. **בין דמוקרטיה ליהדות** (דיון) משרד החינוך והתרבות, ירושלים, תשמ"ח.

4. בלפר א' (עורכת), **מנהיגות רוחנית בישראל**, דביר, ירושלים, תשמ"ב.
5. טל א', **מיתוס ותבונה ביהדות ימינו**, ספרית פועלים, תל-אביב, תשמ"ז.
6. כהן ס', "מושג שלושת הכתרים; מקומו במחשבה היהודית" (תדפיס) בר-אילן, רמת-גן, תשמ"ח.
7. לנגר מ', "דמוקרטיה, דת ועתידנו הציוני", **מבפנים, נ'** (2-1 אביב, תשמ"ח) עמ' 77-86.
8. נוברגר ב', "ישראל — דמוקרטיה ליברלית?", **נקודות תצפית — תרבות וחברה בארץ ישראל**, גרף 1' (עורכת), האונ' הפתוחה, תל-אביב, תשמ"ח, עמ' 105-126.
9. שלזינגר ואחרים (עורכים), **הקיבוץ בהלכה**, שעלבים, תשמ"ד.
10. שבייד א', **דמוקרטיה והלכה**, מאגנס, ירושלים, תשל"ח.
11. הנ"ל, "הדמוקרטיה מול מורשת התרבות היהודית" (תדפיס) כרם, ירושלים, תשמ"ח.

12. D. Elazar, "Covenant as the Basis of the Jewish Political Tradition," in D. Elazar (ed.), *Kinship and Consent: The Jewish Political Tradition and its Uses* (Washington, D.C.: University Press of America, 1983), pp. 1–56.
13. E. Luz, "The Moral Price of Sovereignty: The Dispute about the Use of Power within Zionism," *Modern Judaism*, February, 1987, pp. 51–98.
14. U. Simon, "Religion, Morality and Politics," *Forum* 28–29 (1978), pp. 102–110.
15. U. Tal, "Totalitarian Democratic Hermeneutics and Politics in Modern Jewish Religious Nationalism," in *Totalitarian Democracy and After* (Jerusalem: Magnes Press, 1984), pp. 137–157.

SEMINAR 2
Israel-Diaspora Relations

To some extent, this seminar would overlap with every other seminar. Thus, it would be impossible to conduct a discussion here which did not touch upon the other five areas. Nevertheless, we did need to consider an overall approach to contacts and relations between Diaspora Conservative Jewry and Israelis, Masorti or otherwise. In the latter part of the twentieth century, Jews live freely with sovereignty in the State of Israel and without sovereignty in the Diaspora. How ought each community to view the other? How can relations be strengthened? More specifically, how deeply and how vigorously should Diaspora and Israeli Jewry try to influence the affairs of the other community; and in what areas, and in what ways? For American Conservatism, this broad question devolves into more specific questions: What should we do and what should we say about Israeli foreign policy, about Israeli domestic affairs? To what extent should different rules govern our pronouncements and our actions in each of these areas? What are our special responsibilities as Israel's supporters in American political life? What stances should we take in international Jewish policy-making bodies? What is our position on alternative philanthropic endeavors? Some Israelis have criticized the image of financial dependency encouraged by the major philanthropic drives on Israel's behalf. Some Americans have developed innovative ways of supporting specific sorts of Israeli causes. Do we have a position on these arguments and developments?

Conservative-Masorti Zionism in a Rapidly Changing World

RAPHAEL ARZT

INTRODUCTION

When approaching any problem of Jewish meaning, I try to suspend personal memories, which, while influencing personal life decisions, should not bear on broader ideological discourse.

By doing so, I avoid converting personal attachments and nostalgia into ideological templates, and understanding present conditions in the light of preconceptions generated by memories. I take this position although I treasure the myths in which I was educated and which fostered my own aliyah.

IDEOLOGICAL CONSIDERATIONS

The range of ideological models relating to Israel is great. Various definitions, and elaborations of principles, underlie such ideas as holiness, chosenness, normative Judaism, nationalism, Zionism, movements of liberation, particularism and universalism, egalitarianism, modernity, and postmodernity. Some of these ideas stem from classical sources, some from contemporary sources, and some are still rudimentary and in the process of being formulated.

One's ideological choices result from a meshing of diverse elements into a pattern of meaning which has a tacit and aesthetic appeal. Once chosen, an ideological position is recommended to others to appropriate as their own. Various strategies of presentation and persuasion then express an ideological program, whose success usually is determined much later.

My own ideological position regarding Israel follows the lead of Max Kadushin, *z.l.*[1] I understand Israel as a value concept which stresses the centrality of community, in the conspectus of values comprising a Jewish world-view. Israel's existence underscores most vividly the principle that, wherever Jews live, they are obligated to form communities and communal structures to further the process of personal and collective redemption. Only thus will the spiritual component of Judaism as a civilization be realized, be it in Israel, the United States, or the Soviet Union.

The State of Israel currently offers the richest possibilities for future Jewish communal development. It is rooted in a history-laden territory, Eretz Yisrael, and in a language, Hebrew, both of which resonate with associations that contribute to communal realization. In contrast to other religious world-views, this worldly community-building becomes the means of redemption and of *tikkun olam* (repair of the world) for the Jewish people.

FUTURISTIC CONSIDERATIONS

The Jewish tradition has established the mitzvah of Yishuv Eretz Yisrael (settling in the land of Israel) as a dominant theme. The tradition has expressed its commitment to this mitzvah in such sayings as, "When Jacob is in the land of Israel he has a God, and when he is not in the land of Israel it is as if he is godless."[2] "Settling in the land of Israel is a mitzvah equal to all the other mitzvot together,"[3] and "A wife can force her husband to go to the land of Israel."[4] The Haggadah's declaration, "Next year in Jersualem," Yehudah Halevi's yearning, "My heart is in the east, but I am in the west," and Jeremiah's promise that "thy sons shall return to their borders"[5] likewise unequivocally reflect the Jews' commitment to the Land.

Historically, Jews circumvented this mitzvah only as a result of emerging sociological and geopolitical realities. That Jews did not realize this ideal in the past is a fact of historical reality that does not contradict the idea. Yet reality does more to mold a people's essence than do yearnings and dreams. Yoḥanan ben Zakkai responded to a reality in negotiating a transition from the Temple cult to the Academy at Yavneh. Herzl reacted to contemporary social and political forces to develop a nationalistic solution to the "Jewish problem." Weizmann, Ben-Gurion, and Begin's response to the catastrophic reality of the Holocaust was to bring about the final realization of statehood.

The contemporary debate about two centers to the Jewish people uses the metaphor of "Babylonia and Jerusalem," which is borrowed from a totally different historical setting. The use of such metaphors does not reflect the reality that Diaspora Jews are not flocking to Israel, although two millennia of enforced exile are over. Throughout the ages, the ideal of Yishuv Eretz Yisrael has functioned as a dream but has been largely ignored as a program of action for most of world Jewry.

In terms of my ideological formulation, however, Diaspora Jews have long concretized the value-concept of Israel by forming communities wherever they lived. Those who *did* come to the land of Israel also concretized this value by first forming the Yishuv (organized Jewish community in Palestine) and then a state, both forms of communal organization, appropriate to the needs of the time.

The two-center debate may become academic as a new reality unfolds. One can imagine a world setting twenty-five to fifty years from now in which—

1. access to peoples, places, ideas, and enterprises throughout the world is far easier than today;
2. democratic, pragmatic, and technological problem-solving techniques are appropriated by many peoples, thus forming an efficient, westernized culture of productivity;
3. increased rapid transportation and information-based industries lead to far greater economic and professional mobility;
4. economic and cultural interdependence of peoples throughout the world is the dominant reality;
5. a growing popular individualistic consciousness contributes to a differently perceived balance between the value of personal self-fulfillment and that of communal fulfillment; and
6. there is a natural shift from a theocentric (God-centered)

consciousness to anthropocentric (human-centered) consciousness.

Given this unfolding reality, the communal form of statehood may become less of a generative ideal and continue to exist only as a useful organizational form. It may be replaced by generative ideals that relate more to the *quality* than the *form* of communal life. If so, the theme of two centers will be replaced by interest in the quality of life in a one-world Jewish community dispersed among different "neighborhoods" in a "world city." Such a conception would reintroduce Simon Dubnow's approach to Jewish nationalism, which is spiritual and cultural rather than territorial.

In light of rapidly emerging social and technological realities, many of the basic terms of reference with which we relate to the State of Israel will have to change. Aliyah, yeridah (emigration from Israel), security, Zionist self-fulfillment, and other basic Zionist ideas and movements will be overshadowed by concepts that pertain directly to quality-of-life issues, e.g., the protection of the environment, pluralism, and peace.

Each committed Jew will have to decide what kind of Jewish community to live in, i.e., what mode of neighborhood/communal organization he/she feels is most effective in promoting quality-of-life concerns. A community that offers the most Jewish historical and linguistic resonances, that provides the widest institutional framework for personal and communal realization, may contribute more to Jewish survival and renewal than communities that are minority enclaves in an attractive majority culture. Reasoning thus, a committed Jew may well be prompted to travel across the sea and settle in Israel.

PROGRAMMATIC CONSIDERATIONS

Some practical implications based on the above principles which could guide our movement over the next fifty years are:

1. We should change our terms of reference from "Diaspora-Israel relationship" to concepts that better reflect the spiritual

and cultural concerns of the world Jewish people and its evolving civilization.
2. We should not axiomatically attempt to draw ideological inspiration from the State of Israel as such, only from the people of Israel, whose mission is to build an exemplary communal society in and through the state.
3. We should prepare ourselves for a growing gap of world-views between the State of Israel, which necessarily functions in the world of realpolitik, and other Jewish communities, which do not. States often function in an amoral setting, often having to choose "lesser evils" in complex and murky situations.
4. While Diaspora Jews should express opinions and offer advice on geopolitical issues, they should focus primarily on promoting communal frameworks which enhance Jews' quality of life as defined by our movement.
5. We should create new channels of communication and cooperation which draw disparate communities closer together so as to form a Judaic cultural and spiritual force that is compelling in an ever more pluralistic Jewish world.

NOTES
1. My position is not identical with that of Kadushin, z.l.
2. Tosefta Avodah Zarah, chap. 5.
3. Sifrei Deuteronomy 12:29.
4. B. Ketuvot 110b.
5. Jeremiah 31:16.

To Strengthen Weak Ties: The Conservative Movement and the Country of Israel

STEVEN M. COHEN

In thinking of Israel, many American Jews really feel that "We Are One." The well-known UJA slogan captures the idea that the Jews of the United States, Israel, and elsewhere share a common heritage, condition, and destiny. These three words connote not only a Jew's sense of solidarity with Jews everywhere, they also implicitly argue that all Jews share a quite similar sense of what it means to be Jewish.

Certainly, American and Israeli Jews have much in common. From the Exodus and Mount Sinai to the Holocaust and the founding of the State of Israel, the same historical events inform our collective memories. We celebrate many of the same holidays, practice many of the same customs, respond to many of the same symbols, and engage with many of the same texts. Most Jews around the world see the Jewish people as an extended family, one which has long suffered enormous persecution and remains endangered to this day.

At the same time, very profound differences, which are bound to deepen and widen in the decades ahead, separate the Jews and "Judaisms" of these two societies.

Israelis comprise a Jewish state with the power, responsibilities, and political and moral dilemmas that only are possible in a sovereign state; American Jews comprise a voluntary community as citizens of a multi-ethnic country. Jewish Israelis are a majority in their own society; American Jews are a minority in a society which is demographically and, to a certain extent, culturally Christian. Israelis speak Hebrew, the primary language of Jewish cultural creativity; few American Jews have access to Jewish texts and other cultural resources composed in Hebrew. For the "Jewish mainstreams" in both countries who do not live a life of halakhah, this divergence is particularly telling.

Each of the two major Jewish societies has developed a concept of Judaism that is totally alien to the other. For example, Israelis have made the concept of Eretz Yisrael central to their Judaism. They are fascinated with the Land's history and topography, what grows and lives above it as well as what may be buried beneath it. Religious and secular alike invest Eretz Yisrael with a sacredness that few American Jews recognize, let alone fully comprehend.

For their part, American Jews have come to identify liberalism and progressive social movements with Judaism. A recent *Los Angeles Times* poll asked a nationwide sample of American Jews what Judaism meant to them. Half the sample, including a majority of Conservative Jews, picked "social equality," rejecting by wide margins such choices as "religion" or "Israel." To most American Jews, to be a good Jew still means to be a good liberal. In Israel, liberalism is at best irrelevant to one's Judaism; at worst, it is suspected of signifying alienation from the Jewish tradition.

American Jews revel in their cultural cosmopolitanism; many Israelis, particularly in recent years, reject Western ideas, culture, and literature as irrelevant or even subversive. American Jews are at least rhetorically committed to civil rights and the protection of minorities. Israeli Jews have less to fear from a government that is their own, that is an extension of the "Jewish family." American Jews are generally uncomfortable with the overt assertion of Jewish superiority; Israelis often see the rule of law as subordinate to personal contacts or to higher religious or nationalist principles. Some even have developed what an Israeli social scientist has called a "culture of illegalism." Americans recognize as legitimate several ideological trends with Jewish life; Israelis—even secular ones—generally recognize only Orthodoxy as religiously authoritative and authentic.

The increasing disparity between Israeli and American Judaism constitutes both a problem and an opportunity. It is a problem because it may lead to more intense and deeper strains between Israeli and American Jewish leadership, as well as to greater remoteness between the Israeli and American Jewish masses. If such mutual alienation continues, each Jewish community would be deprived of the political, spiritual, and cultural resource provided by the other, leaving world Jewry much the weaker. But the disparity also presents an educational and spritiual challenge to both Jewries. A serious and mutual cultural interchange between American and Israeli Jews—one where Conservative Judaism can play a critical role—can enrich the Jewish experience of both. But such a process requires a prior recognition of the many differences which inescapably divide us.

Most American Jews are only dimly aware of these differences. For many years, they have tended to think of Israelis as just like themselves, only better, or, sometimes, worse. But few American Jews understand that Jewishly, Israelis are very different from themselves. In fact, even Jews who are very involved in working on Israel's behalf (to say nothing of the larger number who merely identify strongly with the Jewish state) maintain a very narrow relationship with Israel. For most American Jews (even, perhaps especially, pro-Israel activists) the ties with Israel center exclusively around her very real struggle to survive in a hostile world. The dominant image they have of Israel is of a country surrounded by enemies, beset by internal strife, and desperately in need of the American government's continued military, financial, and diplomatic support. They see their role as supporting social services beyond the ability of a state budget strained by defense needs, and providing the political wherewithal to ensure America's truly singular support for the otherwise isolated Jewish state. This survivalist orientation, while intense and sometimes energizing, is excessively narrow, operating only on the political and philanthropic levels. It ignores Israel's spiritual and cultural dimensions and focuses more on dangers to Israel's continuity than on the content of its existence. In short, it fails to truly appreciate and utilize the distinctiveness of Israeli Jewish life.

The pro-Israel activism typical of many well-intentioned American Jews (among whom Conservative Jews are found in great numbers) generally ignores the real debates within Israel that are part of the country's Jewish richness. The Israeli political landscape today is littered with compelling choices over such questions as how to pursue peace and security, what ought to be the role of religion in the public domain, and how Israel should treat its Arab minorities. For the most part, American Jews are ill-prepared to deal with these issues. According to my 1986 National Survey of American Jews, fewer than one-third of a national sample knew that Menachem Begin and Shimon Peres were from different political parties; fewer than one-third knew that Conservative and Reform rabbis could not officiate at weddings. Ignorance of these basic facts signified an even broader ignorance of the major debates of Israeli society. It is fair to say that most American Jews (affiliated Conservative Jews included), even more pro-Israel activists, cannot articulate a particular vision of Israeli society.

In the heady days between the Six-Day War and the Entebbe rescue, when we were all "Zionists," passion for Israel was sustained despite our blissful ignorance of her internal disputes. At this point in American Jewish history, we were ready to embrace Israel as a newly rediscovered symbol of Jewish pride and heroism. The events of those years reinforced the image of valiant Jews standing strong against a hostile world. The Six-Day War (1967), the first mortalities from Arab terrorism (in 1968), the War of Attrition (1969–71), the Munich Massacre (1972), the Yom Kippur War (1973–74), the Rabat Statement (1974), the "Zionism is Racism" resolution (1975), and the Entebbe rescue (1976) all reinforced the image of Israeli "good guys" locked in a struggle for survival with the Arab "bad guys" and their anti-Semitic and anti-Zionist "running dogs" around the world.

But since 1977, events in Israel and the Mideast have presented more complicated images, some of which have disturbed many thoughtful American Jews, particularly political and religious liberals. The last decade or so has seen the rise to prominence of Ariel Sharon and Meir Kahane, a war of choice in Lebanon, religious intolerance and internal strife, and violent clashes between Israeli soldiers and Palestinians in revolt. None of these images is appealing to American Jewry; many are downright alienating, some are repulsive. If the last ten years are any guide to the future, we can expect more unattractive developments in Israel. These kinds of images will alienate large numbers of American Jews, including many Conservative Jews. How shall we respond to the likely projection of an unattractive, illiberal Israel? Some guidelines:

1. We should recognize for ourselves, and emphasize to others, both what we share with Israelis and how the Israeli and American conditions, Israeli and American Jews, and Israeli and American Judaism are very different. For most American Jews, this approach will help them properly interpret seemingly "unsavory" Israeli words and actions. For a select few, an emphasis on Israel's Jewish distinctiveness may begin to lay the conceptual foundation for a commitment to aliyah.

2. We should emphasize that Israel is confronting important and difficult choices about which the Conservative Movement has something to say in terms of its vision of Israeli society. In short, we need to abandon the absolute image of a unified, homogeneous Israel which we unqualifiedly love. Instead, we might view Israel as a text, one that requires engagement and interpretation and that sometimes yields conflicting meanings.

One model for this might be America Orthodox Jews, who outdistance Conservative Jews in every measure of serious Israeli commitment except one (contributions to the UJA; for the sectarian Orthodox, the UJA is an unacceptably "nonsectarian" Jewish charity). While about a quarter of Conservative Jewish college students have been to Israel, more than twice as many Orthodox youngsters have been there. Where less than ten percent of Conservative Jews claim the ability to conduct simple Hebrew conversations, the figure is four times as high among the Orthodox. While only two or three percent of Conservative parents want their children to make aliyah, a quarter of Orthodox parents feel that way. With only ten percent of the American Jewish population, the Orthodox have supplied at least half of American *olim* (new immigrants) in recent years.

The Orthodox have achieved these impressive results not by trying to love all of Israeli society, but by relating in a serious fashion only to their Israeli Orthodox counterparts, to their yeshivot, neighborhoods, and political movements. They do not hesitate to advance their particular vision of Israeli society, a vision that seeks to expand the influence of halakhah as interpreted by the recognized (Orthodox) Israeli rabbinate.

Conservative Jews certainly cannot, and should not, adopt the specifics of the Orthodox way of relating to Israel. But they should take seriously the model of rugged partisanship Orthodoxy offers us. This selective, discerning approach may be contrasted with the historic efforts of the UJA, Israel Bonds, and many Jewish educators to "sell" all of Israel. Conservative Jews today may no longer be ready to "buy" this, but they certainly can "buy into" one or another part of Israel.

Thus, we should explicitly identify and strengthen our ties with those segments of Israeli society with which we have the most in common. Conservative Jews need not support every Israeli pronouncement or official action in order to love Israel. On the issue of religious pluralism, for example, our stand has been very clear. On questions of land, security, and peace, we have been in a tacit alliance with the Labor Zionist camp for the last few years. The cooperation with the Israeli Left on Knesset legislation, our coalition at the World Zionist Congress, the Seminary's honorary doctorate to Shimon Peres, the recent Masorti movement teshuvah (responsum) permitting the return of land for peace, all underscore our movement's greater sympathy for the world-view of Labor Zionism over that of the Revisionists.

Our slow if steady drift into the Labor camp should be explicitly recognized, elaborated, and strengthened. Just as Orthodoxy has come to stand for a hard-line approach to the Palestinians, so should we as a movement come to stand for a moderate policy line. And just as Orthodoxy has its doves, so should we have a hawkish minority. But Conservative lay people should understand that Judaism, as most Conservative Jewish leaders understand it, demands security policies of restraint, pragmatism, and compromise.

3. We should present Conservative Jews with a "neutral ground," a sphere of activity insulated from the divisive struggles over war and peace, and the place of religion in Israeli society. For example, the Jewish Agency's new lay leadership is trying to move

its social service bureaucracy in a more managerial, less political direction. Conservative Jewish leaders should support such efforts, so that the Jewish Agency, supported by UJA dollars, itself achieves "neutral ground."

4. We should establish a relationship with Israel beyond the political and philanthropic, to new realms of mutual enrichment. For example, we career-minded American Jews can learn something from Israelis' extraordinary commitment to family and friends. Despite Israelis' understandably frenetic pursuit of economic security, the Israeli calendar provides for huge blocks of family time. Evening meetings are rare; the workday ends early; on school holidays, children often "invade" their parents' workplaces. Friday afternoon through Saturday nights are reserved for family and friends; careerism is an infrequently chosen option, and commitment to diligent work habits is widely viewed as a Central European and Anglo-Saxon curiosity. These attitudes—seeing work as an instrument, and family happiness as paramount—draw on a time-honored Jewish tradition, which perhaps can be learned and adapted by American Jewry.

But cultural bridges should extend in both directions. Conservative Jews should proudly communicate to Israelis a commitment to religious tolerance and pluralism, concern for civil liberties and sensitivity to vulnerable minorities, experience with voluntary philanthropy and communal service, and dedication to equal opportunities for men and women. Perhaps most critically, they have valuable experience in approaching the Jewish tradition and adapting it meaningfully to the modern world. Thus, we need to seek ways of importing and exporting the better elements of our Jewish lives.

As Conservative Jews become more aware of the very complicated reality of Israel, we will need to adjust our thinking, programming, and education. With Israel fiercely debating fundamental moral decisions, calls for American Jews unequivocally to support Israel, rather than take informed stands on its most compelling issues, are both impractical and counterproductive. Impractical because to "support" an often-divided Israel, one must back one or another approach to the major problems it faces. Counterproductive because intense involvement with Israel demands that one make intelligent, informed choices.

As opposed to those who contend that American Jews should steer clear of the controversies of Israeli public policy, the Conservative Movement should encourage Conservative Jews to become intimately involved with the struggle over the Jewish State's future, both under the movement's auspices and elsewhere. Alternative philanthropies, support for political movements, and public pronouncements in media which reach large numbers of American Jews may deepen the American Jewish connection with Israel, and enrich Jewish public discourse.

SUMMARY

1. The Conservative Movement should not only emphasize the bonds that unite Jews outside of Israel with those living in the Jewish State, but also recognize the many ways Israeli Jewish life differs dramatically from Diaspora Jewish life.

2. We should recognize that Israel presents us with numerous choices. If we want American Jews to become very committed to Israel, we have to expect them to develop and express positions on controversial issues that confront the Israeli public. Specifically, we should encourage American Jews to "take sides," to become involved in Israel's debates on basic policy questions.

3. We should more forthrightly articulate a Conservative vision of Israel's future. Many leaders of the movement already have developed close ties, even as it encourages the formation of groups within the movement which share a different vision of Israel's future.

4. We should encourage the development of a "neutral zone," a sphere of pro-Israel activity that is relatively insulated from divisive conflicts over Israel's future. Insofar as the Jewish Agency abandons the political for a civil service model, the Conservative Movement should publicize and promote such developments.

5. We need to expand the relationship of American Jews to Israel beyond the philanthropic and political spheres. The relationship should be two-sided; not only should we learn from Israelis, but we also should contribute some of our own insights and achievements to Israeli society.

Ways to Deepen Conservative "Israel Consciousness"

PAUL FREEDMAN

I.

Relationship implies responsibility. However, we must acknowledge that the Diaspora and Israel are not equal. We dare not ignore the theological implications of *Ki mi-Tzion teytze Torah u-devar HaShem mi-Yerushalayim* ("for from Zion came Torah, and the words of God from Jerusalem").

Diaspora (and especially American) Jewry should consider performing *teshuvah* (repentance/return) vis-à-vis its relationship with the State of Israel. The painful reality is that at least eighty percent of North American Jewry have *never visited Israel*. In 1987 and 1988, non-Jewish North Americans, as well as European Jews and non-Jews, were in evidence in Israel. Too many of us were not. An absentee movement can make no impact on, and can in turn not be affected by, Israel.

Because Conservative Judaism is a halakhic movement, our relationship with Israel must be governed by halakhic considerations. We cannot escape the significance of *mitzvot ha-teluyot ba-arez*, the mitzvot that can be practiced only in Israel. Judaism outside Israel is necessarily incomplete.

The *Oxford English Dictionary* derives "Diaspora" from the Greek word meaning "to disperse." It also cites a verse from *Parsha Ki Tavo:* "God will cause you to be smitten before your enemies. On one road will you go out against him, and on seven roads will you flee from him, and you will be a horror to all the kingdoms of the earth'' (Deuteronomy 28:25). The implications of these strong words are clear.

II.

After two thousand years of waiting, the Diaspora may not really want Israel. Our aim must be to change this.

We have much to gain by working within the existing Zionist institutions in both North America and Israel. While we may have many legitimate criticisms of such bodies as the World Zionist Organization/Jewish Agency, we can effect change only to the degree that we participate and play a leadership role in them.

Our movement only very recently has emerged as a Zionist force. The gratifying cooperation by all arms of the movement in approaching WZO/Jewish agency allocations with one voice illustrates how much we have to gain by working together.

In its relationship to Israel, the Conservative Movement is still, however, a sleeping giant; it is just beginning to flex its muscles. Members of our movement occupy key roles in many of the major North American Jewish organizations. To a greater degree than previously, we must tap their energies and expertise in promoting our interests vis-à-vis Israel.

Yet there also is truth to the assertion that one who does not put his life on the line does not have the same rights of expression and determination. Nonetheless, if *kol Yisrael arevim zeh la-zeh* (''all Israel is responsible for each other''), we *do* have some basic right to express ourselves, provided we do so with love and respect and in the proper forum (which does not include the pages of the *New York Times*).

For their part, Israelis should realize that only God is perfect, and that constructive criticism can lead to stronger national development and greater security. Again, provided we do so in an appropriate way, we have an obligation to express our views on both Israeli domestic and foreign affairs. If my Israeli sisters and brothers stand on the borders in a fight for survival, then the mitzvah of *pikku'aḥ nefesh* (saving a human life) is involved in everything we say and do concerning the State of Israel.

One implication of this is that our movement should do everything possible to support Israel's interests on the North American political scene. Our constructive criticism will be viewed with more respect if we make it clear, by word and deed, by opinion pieces, lobbying, and votes, that we are totally committed to Israel's survival and growth. At the same time, we must continue to insist upon equity of process and funding for Conservative institutions and projects in Israel. We certainly should not provide funding to institutions which call for our abolition as a movement.

Israeli educational institutions and programs can benefit from our input. We should not be afraid to suggest ways of improving them, which would also redound to our benefit. At the same time, we should not lose sight of how we need Israel. Our movement cannot close its eyes to the very real problems of the Diaspora. The rates of interdating and intermarriage, and the lack of a full Jewish education by our laity, proclaim that we are in trouble. What better source of renewal have we than the land of Zion and Jerusalem?

There may well be truth in the rabbinic adage that *avirat Eretz Yisrael mahkimah,* "the air of Israel makes one wiser." If we could bring each member of the Conservative Movement to Israel for an in-depth educational and religious program, "Israel-Diaspora relations" would take on a far deeper meaning.

III.

The above is no "impossible dream." To implement it, the movement should consider:

1. A think-tank including representatives from each arm of our movement, to meet semi-annually (once in Jerusalem and once in New York) to explore ways of deepening the Israel-Diaspora connection. This format would permit more open-ended, less institution-bound, "brainstorming" than is presently the case. The think-tank also might discuss ways and means of bringing more North American Conservative Jews to Israel, and ways of positively influencing the Israeli informal and formal educational systems. A wide variety of Con-

servative and Masorti bodies would have responsibility for implementing the recommendations both here and in Israel.
2. Increasing the number of *sheliḥim* (representatives of Israeli institutions in the Diaspora) working within the movement's congregations, day schools, and youth programs. The presence of knowledgeable *sheliḥim* might not only increase knowledge of Israel but also strengthen basic Judaic knowledge and practice among our undereducated laity.
3. Undertaking a campaign to increase lay participation in Zionist enterprises and dialogues, including local Zionist organizations. The Conservative Movement's leadership is crucial to revitalizing North American Zionism.
4. Requiring Conservative organizations to increase dramatically visits to Israel in 1989, 1990, and beyond.
5. Declaring 5750 (1989–90) as *shenat ha-aretz* ("year of the land"), with programs in Israel and North America organized by every arm of the movement.
6. Undertaking a massive enrollment campaign for membership in Mercaz, so as to give added weight to our Zionist voice. This should be done without impinging upon the autonomy of any constituent member organization.
7. Developing a program for bringing successfully integrated North American *olim* who are members of the Masorti Movement to meet with Conservative Jews here on Israel/Diaspora relations and aliyah.
8. Producing a regular newsletter to inform our constituency of Conservative/Masorti positions on current issues. The newsletter should represent divergent viewpoints within the movement.

The Ongoing Importance of the Diaspora

DAVID LIEBER

Since the establishment of the State of Israel, the relationship between it and the American Jewish community has been warm and close, to the benefit of both. For American Jewry, Israel has been a source of pride and renewed vitality. Israel, in turn, has depended on American Jewish political and financial support to help build its infrastructure, absorb hundreds of thousands of new settlers, and defend itself against invading Arab armies. American Jewish life has been enriched immeasurably by Israeli scholarship and creativity, while American olim and well-wishers have contributed their expertise toward the development of Israel's economy and the American Jewish community has influenced the American government to support the Jewish state.

Of late, "cracks" have begun to appear in the relationship, resulting in part from political decisions taken by the Israel government, and in part from its citizens' apparently growing indifference to democratic values. American Jews also have matured in their attitudes towards Israel; they now view it as a flesh-and-blood reality, not predominantly as a symbol of Jewish heroism and superhuman achievement. They have come to be concerned that Israelis do not seem to care about *their* sensitivities or interests, as demonstrated by the continuing denigration of the Reform and Conservative movements, and the recent Pollard spy case. Many Israelis, even those as sophisticated as Shlomo Avineri, are quick to suggest that American Jewish leaders have a Galut mentality and, by inference, should refrain from criticizing Israeli foreign and security policies in public forums.

During the past months, tensions between the two communities have become exacerbated as American Jews have debated the propriety of bringing pressure on Israel to alter its policies towards the Palestinian Arabs. Some, like Rita Hauser and Rabbi Alexander Schindler, insist that American Jews must speak out and exert whatever influence they can to keep Israel from what they view as a diastrous policy that violates "the Jewish sense of justice." Others, like Morris Abrams, urge caution in order to avoid "splitting the Jewish camp," thus providing Israel's enemies with an opening to press for reducing American aid.

Neither side seems to have convinced the other, an impasse that reflects the dilemma of contemporary American Jews who care deeply about the Jewish people. On the one hand, they recognize that there is some justice in the claim of Israeli government leaders that only those who accept the burdens and responsibilities of citizenship have a right to determine Israel's policies. On the other, they believe that as Jews they have a personal stake not only in the survival of the state, but in its character, and so cannot ignore what is happening there.

Aliyah, the classical Zionist appeal to all who love the Land of Israel, and are seriously committed to securing the Jewish future, is one way out of this impasse. Among aliyah's virtues is that it enables one to participate personally in realizing the millennial dream of the Jewish people. It has not, however, been a realistic approach for the entire community; in the forty years of Israel's existence, fewer than one percent of America's Jews have attempted it. Since this is true of the generation that witnessed the Holocaust, a horrendous confirmation of the Herzlian thesis that Diaspora Jews are in mortal danger, it is unlikely that others will opt for aliyah in the foreseeable future.

This is not surprising, since Diaspora living has been part of the Jewish experience for at least twenty-five hundred years. Since the Babylonian exile, Judaism, while "land-centered," has not been "land-bound." One can argue that the disappearance of the Diaspora would be a great blow to the Jewish people and a loss to the whole world. It is a fact that the symbiotic relationships between Jews and other peoples among whom they have lived have enriched both Jewish culture and other civilizations. There is every reason to believe that this will remain the case, provided vibrant Diaspora Jewish communities can be maintained.

Our central concern, then, should be more than the strengthening of the State of Israel; it should be the creative survival of the Jewish people. This requires not alone its physical well-being, but a regeneration of the Jewish spirit through nourishment from its tradition and openness to modern values and insights.

In this Israel can play a leading role. It has generated enthusiasm among world Jewry for its remarkable achievements in "ingathering the exiles" and in building an advanced industrial society in the face of incredible odds. It should also demonstrate how classic Jewish values may be applied to running a modern state that is both sensitive to ethical issues and protective of its citizens' security and interests.

For its part, the Diaspora should serve not merely as a hinterland for the Israeli "motherland," but as an independent partner in shaping the Jewish ethos and deriving from it personal enrichment and inspiration. It can be a valuable ally even to a State of Israel at peace with its neighbors by sharing the state's perspectives and insights and by extending its cultural "reach" throughout the world.

The above model clearly rejects the classical Zionist notion of "negating the Diaspora." It certainly does not see the dismemberment of the Diaspora in favor of the State of Israel as a worthy goal. It assumes the possibility of ongoing Diaspora Jewish life despite the well-known problems it faces; it views the Diaspora as important in its own right. This perspective requires taking our religious, cultural, and educational institutions much more seriously than we have to date. We must provide funds to train more sophisticated professional leaders, educate the laity, encourage greater creativity in the arts, radically upgrade communications systems, maintain first-rate educational institutions, and design compelling Israel programs for the Diaspora. Only a dynamic, Jewishly literate Diaspora—at home in the classics and knowledgeable in both Jewish history and contemporary Jewish affairs (and, one hopes, conversant in Hebrew)—can serve as a genuine partner in Israel. Only with this type of Diaspora will it be possible to "build bridges" between Israel and the other great Jewish centers. As a friend recently pointed out, one can only build a bridge between two fixed bases, not between one that is firm and one that is shaky.

This model does *not* imply that the contribution of Diaspora communities, including the American one, is as important as Israel's in furthering Jewish life. It is extremely doubtful that the American Jewish community is capable of the same type of creativity that characterized Babylonia during the rabbinic age. Nevertheless, it is inappropriate to describe Israel as "central" and the Diaspora as "peripheral," since it suggests that the "center" can function without the "periphery," and need not necessarily be concerned with it. A much better metaphor is the one offered by Nathan Rotenstreich, who speaks of "the primacy" of Israel.[1] Israel occupies a primary position in Jewish life because it is the focus of worldwide Jewish concerns and because one can experience Jewishness there in many more positive ways than in the Diaspora.

We should think of the centrality of the Jewish people, with Israel as but one instrument in serving it, albeit the primary one. Since Israel, like the Diaspora communities, serves a larger purpose, it has to be as concerned about world Jewry's welfare as they are of its. It has to take into account their needs and interests in formulating its policies and avoid taking steps which threaten its solidarity with them.

Diaspora leaders, while respecting the integrity and sovereignty of the state, should feel free to criticize those actions which threaten to alienate them from it, particularly when their interests or deeply held values are involved. As in every family relationship, mutual respect and openness are absolutely essential if estrangement is to be avoided. This may lead to occasional public acrimony, but that is far preferable to the disaffection which inevitably results when grievances are not aired and given due consideration.

Ultimately, both Israel and American Jewry are "free agents" and will act as such. To avoid major misunderstandings, major Jewish communities must create improved channels of communication and consultation. Even this will not be enough if both communities do not make the effort to really understand each other's needs and aspirations. It is crucial that both Israelis and Diaspora Jews struggle to grasp differences in their perceptions and values. While such differences may not always be reconcilable, understanding and articulating them will help each community avoid misunderstandings. Israelis should be aware of Americans' concerns for pluralism and the separation of church and state, while Americans must understand a society in which many citizens are only one generation away from the premodern world. They also should appreciate the security factors that compel the Israeli government to engage in political brinkmanship.

In the final analysis Jewish solidarity will depend on maintaining a sense of a common destiny and shared vision. The Conservative Movement can make an important contribution, since it speaks the language of both tradition and modernity. Its experience of translating traditional wisdom into a contemporary idiom can help fill the spiritual void many secular Israelis have felt since the Yom Kippur War. The Masorti Movement can help create a common vocabulary for the various ethnic and religious groups through—

- symposia and publications involving both Israeli opinion-makers and thoughtful American Jews;
- extensive adult education programs and materials;
- the judicious use of the mass media;
- the training of capable Israeli rabbis, teachers, group workers, and writers.

Simultaneously, the Conservative Movement should educate its laity to engage in an ongoing, fruitful relationship with Israel. Aliyah should be held up as a viable option for people eager to assist in bringing "modern traditional Judaism" to Israel. For those unwilling or unable to make a lifetime commitment to living in Israel, the movement should establish a program for relatively short-term (six months to three years) programs of service there, similar to those sponsored by the American government for overseas service.

Mordecai Kaplan once observed that the only heresy Judaism

cannot tolerate is ignorance. To battle that "heresy," we must bridge the gap between Israel and the Diaspora, so as to ensure that our great-grandchildren will still see themselves as belonging to one people.

SUMMARY

Forty years after the establishment of the State of Israel, the relationship between it and the American Jewish community remains undefined. While desirable, aliyah is not a realistic option for most American Jews. Barring unforeseen circumstances, the disappearance of the Diaspora in the next few generations is neither likely nor desirable. A vibrant Diaspora is important for the creative survival of the Jewish people, which should be the central concern both of Israel and Diaspora communities. Thus, one should not speak of the "centrality" of Israel, but of its "primacy," since both Israel and the Diaspora must be concerned with the other's well-being. This requires regular interaction between them which can only take place if organized channels of communication are established and they learn to speak a common language. The Conservative Movement can prove to be especially helpful here, since it has much experience in translating the language of tradition into a modern idiom. Because "bridge-building" requires strong anchor points on both sides, the movement has its work cut out for it.

NOTE

1. "The Present-Day Relationship of State and Diaspora," in *World Jewry and the State of Israel,* edited by M. Davis, (New York: Arno Press, 1977), p. 335.

SEMINAR 3

The Role of Religion in Israel

The Masorti Movement has developed the beginning of a distinctive approach to the matter of religion in Israel. On the one hand, we want to foster and help shape the emergence of a non-Orthodox religious sensibility in Israel. For this reason, we reject the unalloyed secularism of many political and intellectual elements in Israel society. On the other hand, we want to limit the use of state power either to coerce religious conformism or to deny the free exercise and development of non-Orthodox Judaic tendencies.

If, in fact, the foregoing paragraph expresses in approximate terms a philosophical consensus in the movement (and, of course, this assumption bears critical examination), what are the programmatic and practical implications of such a philosophy? We should ask ourselves some tough questions. For example: Where do we stand on conversions and the issue of "Who is a Jew?" We naturally reject all legislative attempts to delegitimize conversions by Conservative rabbis, but do we really want to (and need to) endorse acceptance of conversions by Reform rabbis that violate halakhah? More generally, what sorts of relations ought we to maintain with the Reform Movement in Israel and with our secularist political allies in and around the Israeli Labor Party?

To take another and undoubtedly more critical issue, how much autonomy should the Masorti Movement exercise relative to Diaspora Conservatism? On the one hand, we want the Masorti Movement to be vigorous and vibrant, and that may demand considerable freedom of action and thought. On the other hand, we want to maintain the integrity of a worldwide Conservative Movement. In light of these competing goals, what sorts of consultation and relationships should rabbinical and lay readers in Israel and the Diaspora undertake?

Strategies for the Conservative/ Masorti Movement

CHARELS S. LIEBMAN

DEFINING TERMS

The meaning of "The Role of Religion in Israel" is hardly self-evident. The phrase is clear enough in a discussion of American society, where it would probably deal with Judaism, Catholicism, Protestantism, and new religious movements in the United States. Since it probably never occurred to anybody that this paper would deal with Christianity and Islam in Israel, the topic "Religion in Israel" translates into "Judaism in Israel." The Orthodox would be very comfortable with this kind of formulation. Not only do they equate Orthodoxy with Judaism; within Orthodox circles, attacks on religion are labeled as anti-Semitic. It is not unusual to hear newspapers such as *Ha-Aretz* and the *Jerusalem Post*, Israeli television, or Knesset members such as Shulamit Aloni described as anti-Semites.

The mass media and many Israeli politicians are guilty of bias and distortion in portraying religion and the religious establishment. But the equation of such bias and distortion with anti-Semitism not only suggests that the media, or some political leaders, hate Orthodox Jews (I'm not even certain that this is a fair generalization) but that there is no distinction between Orthodoxy and Judaism. I hope that Conservative/Masorti Jews make such distinctions. Orthodoxy is a particular interpretation of the Jewish tradition which arose in the eighteenth and nineteenth centuries in response to the challenge of modernization. One may argue, quite properly in my opinion, that Orthodoxy is a more faithful reproduction of the religious tradition out of which it emerged, and more faithful to the halakhic process, than is Conservatism. But it is hardly identical with the religious tradition, much less with Judaism.

The founders of modern Zionism, particularly the intellectual elite, harbored ambiguous feelings about the Jewish tradition (which is what I think most of us mean in using the term "Judaism"). Like all modern nationalisms, Jewish nationalism sought to anchor its vision of the future in a national history and culture. It defined itself as a legitimate heir of the Jewish past and as the authentic representative of contemporary Jews. This assertion would have been vitiated had Zionists admitted their alienation from the tradition. On the other hand, Zionist leaders were conscious of the enmity which most religious leaders harbored toward them and their objectives (this they sought to overcome by appeasement, cooperation, and deception). Yet they were also aware of the fact that the Jewish tradition included elements of passivity, fatalism, and otherworldliness that presented an important obstacle in transforming the personality of the Jew, an objective which most Zionist leaders shared. The Zionists' solution was to redefine Judaism as essentially national and secular. Diaspora Judaism, according to its conception, adopted a religious form to preserve the Jews' framework after the destruction of the Temple. But now that Jews had returned to the Land of Israel they could, and should, reaffirm the national rather than the religious essence of Judaism.

This interpretation of Judaism, which was once prevalent in school curricula and among intellectuals and the political elite, has declined dramatically in the past twenty to thirty years. Even those who are "secular Jews" no longer believe that Judaism can be properly understood or experienced without its religious dimension. The late Yaacov Rabi, a writer for the Mapam daily *Al ha-Mishmar,* reflected this position when he said, "Those who believe that secular Judaism is Judaism minus religion are wrong. Judaism minus religion is nothing." Survey data suggest that less than ten percent of the Israeli Jewish population believes that Judaism can be properly interpreted without a religious dimension.

Yet most Jews in Israel do not believe that Judaism and the Jewish religion are synonymous. Like Jews all over the world, they have difficulty defining Judaism. But survey data and my own impressions suggest that most Israeli Jews agree that Judaism is a culture with a strong religious component which links the past and contemporary Jews, and which requires a certain fidelity to the past. It is not simply a code of religious law, a set of beliefs, and a library of sacred texts, as many Orthodox Jews would have it.

Conversely, Judaism in Israel is also *not* defined by what Israelis or Israeli Jews do, as a number of secular intellectuals would have it. There is a strong religious dimension to Jewish culture—for example, the belief in God and in a special relationship between Him and the Jewish people. Other dimensions of this conception of Judaism include Jewish history, Jewish literature, and Jewish ethnicity (a sense of family among Jews), a Jewish homeland (Eretz Yisrael), and perhaps, Jewish statehood.

To most Israelis, the religious dimensions may overlap these other dimensions but they also exist independently of the Jewish religion. Thus, one can be a Jew, perhaps even a good Jew, without necessarily being religious. It is much less clear to most Israeli Jews whether one can be a religious Jew without being Orthodox, i.e., without being faithful to halakhah. Likewise, many Israelis wonder whether one can be faithful to halakhah without the legitimization of those leaders acknowledged by the Orthodox establishment.

The term "Orthodox" or "Orthodoxy" is almost never used in Israel. When an Israeli says he is *dati* (roughly, twenty percent of Israeli Jews so define themselves), Americans who think they are familiar with Israeli society interpret this to mean "Orthodox." Thus, a distinguished American Conservative figure stated last year that, were he living in Israel, he would not define himself as *dati*. But that statement ignores the Israeli cultural context in which the term is used. True, the closest American equivalent to a *dati* Israeli is an Orthodox Jew. But this can be very misleading. To an Israeli, to be *dati* means to believe in God, to be concerned with what He wants of humans in general and Jews in particular, and, most significantly, to observe Jewish law. To not be *dati* means either to be *ḥiloni* (secular), which suggests that the whole matter of religion is unimportant, or to be *masorati* (traditional). The latter, the most amorphous of all categories, generally connotes one who observes some, but not all, Jewish law out of a sense of identification with the Jewish past rather than from a strong belief that a Jew is commanded to do so.

The adoption by the Conservative Movement in Israel of the term Masorti (a variation of *masorati*) seems to me a mistake, primarily because to be *masorati* (traditional) is, almost by definition, to lack precise Jewish ideological and behavioral standards. There is nothing particularly positive about being *masorati,* which simply means that one is neither *dati* nor *ḥiloni*. Israelis confess to being *masorati;* they are not necessarily proud of it. It is thus not surprising that the proportion of Israelis who define themselves as *masorati* is declining. In other words, in the context of Israeli typologies of religious identity, to state that one is not *dati* is to admit that one does not take with utmost seriousness religious imperatives and the religious tradition.

STRATEGIES FOR THE CONSERVATIVE-MASORATI MOVEMENT

One more viable strategy for the Conservative-Masorti Movement would define itself as concerned with all aspects of Judaism; nothing Jewish or Judaic would be foreign to it. It might then see its role as educating Israeli Jews about the nature of Judaism (there is not only a great deal of ignorance about Judaism among many Israeli Jews, but a desire to learn more), of course expressing its own distinct interpretation of Judaism.

I question this strategy. There are a number of public and private organizations in Israel that devote themselves to increasing Jewish knowledge and commitment among Israelis. Many of them have proven successful in awakening public interest, but few have succeeded in evoking any real commitment. To generate commitment and a sense of purpose, it is not enough to inform people what Judaism is; one must also inform them about how Jews are obliged to behave. People don't come to synagogues to learn about their heritage, although that can and should be a by-product of synagogue attendance. If people are interested primarily in acquiring knowledge they can do so more effectively outside the synagogue. I also don't believe that the Conservative-Masorti Movement is faithful to its mission or builds on its real strengths by projecting itself in this fashion. On the other hand, there is no reason for the movement to eschew any aspect of Judaism or Jewish life where it feels it has something to contribute.

A second strategy for the Conservative-Masorti Movement is to project itself as a specifically religious movement. The movement can confront the present religious (Orthodox) establishment, challenging its interpretation of Jewish law and its monopoly of the term *dati*. Alternatively, the movement can ignore the present religious establishment and provide a different conception of what it means to be a religious Jew.

What does challenging the religious establishment mean? Is there really such an entity at all in Israel? After all, at least a quarter of the *datiim* are *haredim* (ultra-Orthodox) who do not recognize the authority of the Chief Rabbinate and its institutions. They also are disdainful of Religious Zionism's most precious symbols—the memory and heritage of Rav Kook, the religious significance of the State of Israel, and the religious responsibility of serving Israeli society. Since *haredi* religious leaders enjoy a large measure of authority among Religious Zionists, the problematics of referring to a religious establishment is clear. In addition, the *haredi* community is bitterly divided by periodic intracommunal charges of heresy and by occasional outbreaks of violence. Nevertheless, the vast majority of Israelis certainly have an image, which is generally negative, of a religious establishment.

There also is a religious bureaucracy of sorts. It controls the Ministry of Religion, parts of the Ministry of the Interior and the Ministry of Education, the religious courts, the local religious councils, and the national and local offices of the Chief Rabbis. This bureaucracy is by no means cut of one cloth and even varies in terms of party and personal loyalties. But it is united in vigorous opposition to any deviation from the religious norms it shares and in its opposition to a non-Orthodox presence in Israel. Thus, the strategy of attacking the Orthodox establishment, and of projecting the Masorti Movement as its mirror image in its understanding of Judaism, is a tempting one.

In pursuing such a strategy, the movement would emphasize that it is a halakhic movement whose understanding of Jewish law differs from that of the religious establishment. Such a strategy might dictate that the movement *not* oppose the proposed amendment to the Law of Return, mandating the acceptance only of converts "according to halakhah."

I don't propose that the movement adopt such a strategy now. Too much emotional energy has been invested, and lines between the sides are too clearly drawn, for the Conservative-Masorti Movement to reassess its position on the issue. Furthermore, the damage has been done.

But in principle the initial opposition to the amendment may have been a mistake, for it placed the Conservative-Masorti Movement in the peculiar position of justifying conversions that are *not* in accordance with halakhah. Instead, the movement might have argued that it had no objection to amending the Law of Return to exclude non-halakhic conversions. But if such an amendment passed, the movement would insist that those converted by Conservative rabbis be recognized as Jews, since such conversions are indeed halakhic. It is difficult to imagine such an argument being rejected by the Israeli Supreme Court, unless the very premises of the argument are false.

In such a case, the Conservative-Masorti Movement would have a magnificent public forum to make clear that it is distinguishable from Reform by its observance of halakhah, and is being unreasonably maligned by the religious establishment. Instead, the Conservative-Masorti leadership chose to align itself with the Reform Movement, in the role of junior partner at that, leaving a public impression that its conversions are no different than Reform ones. I hope that this impression is mistaken. If not, I suggest that the Conservative Movement had better clean up its own house.

There are other instances where declarations by the religious establishment offer opportunities for the Masorti Movement to affirm an independent halakhic position, most notably in terms of rights of women. Adopting the above strategy, however, constitutes a claim that the Masorti Movement does accept the binding nature of halakhah and has a battery of qualified halakhic decisors who can offer alternative halakhic opinions as the need arises. This may require that the movement subsidize a number of rabbis and teachers to devote a good part of their time to the formulation of halakhic opinions.

Another strategy, by no means exclusive of the above, is the development of the non-halakhic aspects of the Jewish religion. Such a strategy means the projection of Judaism as the set of rituals, myths, symbols, ideas, and beliefs that center around questions of ultimate human concerns. It may be particularly amenable to a congregational rabbi and be particularly attractive to many non-*datiim*. As Israelis become more concerned with questions of personal meaning, they are increasingly open to messages that speak to their human concerns. As projected in the schools (both religious and nonreligious) and in the synagogues, Judaism has a great deal to say about a collective past and collective contemporary concerns, but very little to say about individual concerns besides the demands of halakhah. Those rabbis who speak to the individual and his or her concerns are rare exceptions. Israeli Jews are not accustomed to hearing that Judaism has something to say about family relations, old age, loneliness, sickness, or joy. They are generally unaware of how relevant such "theological" concepts as sin, repentance, commandment, or prayer can be to the life and daily routine of an individual who thinks of himself as nonreligious. By emphasizing such matters, the movement bypasses the religious establishment and creates a new model for religion in Israel.

One should not pretend that there will soon be a mass movement of Masorti Jews. Jews who take halakhah seriously are attracted to Orthodoxy. Jews who don't take halakhah seriously do not take religion seriously, but have the option of Reform Judaism. There are no social pressures to join a synagogue in Israel. Hence, there is little motivation to reformulate the synagogue and the service to satisfy religiously marginal Jews. But I don't believe that the potential "market," least of all the short-run market, should be decisive in the movement's considerations. Rather, it is important that Masorti Jews have their own framework to satisfy their religious needs, and that Israeli society have religious alternatives to Orthodoxy.

ON RELATIONS BETWEEN THE CONSERVATIVE AND MASORTI MOVEMENTS

Whatever the present relationship between the Conservative Movement in the United States and the Masorti Movement in Israel, the Israeli movement must have a measure of independence. If it is to grow and make a serious contribution to Israeli Jewish life (and to the Diaspora as well), Masorti must respond to the rhythms and spirit of Israeli society.

Tactically, there may be occasions when it is best for the two branches to adopt separate policies. American Jews often do not understand the nature of Israeli society. More significantly, the Conservative Movement in the United States, addressing its own peculiar issues, may adopt policies about which the Masorti Movement should not have to feel defensive or apologetic. This is especially true in the area of halakhah, where the Masorti Movement, like the Progressive (Reform) Movement in Israel, necessarily retains greater fidelity to the tradition.

Another area in which the Conservative and Masorti Movements may diverge includes the centrality of Israel, of the land and the state, in Judaism. It is natural for the Conservative Movement in the United States to view the state, the land, and even the community of Israel differently than does the Masorti Movement. Thus, it would be foolhardy, indeed, for the Masorti Movement to feel bound by the American movement's ideological formulations. Conversely, the American movement should not feel that is must compromise its convictions because of the potential damage this will cause to the Masorti Movement in Israel.

The Conservative Movement and Israel

STANLEY RABINOWITZ

Although Theodor Herzl and Zadoc Cohen, the Orthodox Chief Rabbi of France, maintained friendly relations, the Chief Rabbi would not give his blessings to Zionism because, "If the state is theocratic as it once was, what will become of freedom of thought? And if it is a secular state, how will it be Jewish?"[1] In other words, the Chief Rabbi could not conceive of a Jewish State that would not be governed by halakhah, but if it were so regulated, how could the state endure? In the forty-first year of the state's existence, Zadoc Cohen's dilemma has yet to be resolved.

We must recognize that a modern society cannot function according to an ancient code of law which is immutable. The Conservative Movement, both within and outside of the State of Israel, should take the lead in reconciling contemporary needs with the requirements of Jewish law. This posture presupposes that the halakhah, as presently interpreted by the dominant religious authorities in Israel, does not and cannot cope with the cataclysmic changes that have occurred in the world, including the Jewish world, since the redaction of the *Shulḥan Arukh* (seventeenth century).

The halakhic regimen which today governs the State of Israel was appropriate to a world in which—

1. Jews were everywhere an oppressed minority;

2. a large number of non-Jews were available to perform duties which Jews could not perform on the Sabbath and festivals; and
3. the secular state provided those services which Jews and others required for their welfare: police, army, sanitation, and a civil service.

None of these conditions prevails in Israel today.

Professor Yeshayah Leibowitz, the iconoclastic Orthodox scholar who is one of the few Israeli intellectuals to grapple with Israel's religious conflicts, has pointed out that the *Shulḥan Arukh* considered neither the possibility nor the needs of a totally Jewish society. Joseph Karo, its compiler, worked in the security of his study in Safed, knowing that he could depend upon the Turkish pasha in Acre to protect the city from enemy attacks, and upon a Turkish police force to protect him and his property from violence. Small wonder that Karo's code contained no rulings to guide a Jewish police force, army, or fire department.

Today, Israelis who observe halakhah can rest securely in their homes on the Sabbath because other Jews, serving in the police force and army, will protect them. They do not deprive themselves of water or electricity (even though the latter may not be switched on or off) on the Sabbath because other Jews maintain the system.

When adjustments in halakhah have been instituted, this has occurred through "legal fictions," the pretense being that the letter of the law has been upheld even though its intent has been clearly violated. Instituting change by this means really involves an evasion of the law. Of all the methods devised to repeal an outmoded law, legal fiction is the most primitive.

In implementing *Shemittah* (the biblical requirement that the land lie fallow every seventh year, a requirement which framed the first conflict between the settlers of the First Aliyah and the upholders of halakhah in 1889), the Chief Rabbinate conveys title to the entire land of Israel to a Gentile during the seventh year. At the end of the year, the land is repurchased. The need to resort to legal fictions to adapt the tradition only underscores the need for its amendment. When applied to the possession of *ḥametz* (leavened bread or other goods) during Passover, change by legal fiction may be regarded as quaint and harmless, but to apply this method to the land of a sovereign state is quite preposterous.

For El Al, the national air line, neither halakhah nor legal fiction can justify flights during holy days: thus, the airline is closed on the Sabbath and festivals. This hardly commends El Al to the non-Jew or to the nonobservant Jewish traveler. Other industries which are dependent upon operating seven days a week, such as chemical plants and automated factories, may seek a certificate of exemption permitting operations on the Sabbath. Not all such requests are granted.

Some learned, respected Orthodox Jewish thinkers, including the late Rabbis Fishman Maimon and Meir Berlin, have advocated amending halakhah to make it more responsive to contemporary needs, either by reestablishing a Sanhedrin or by rabbinic decrees *(takkanot)*. Others have advocated expanding the principle of *pikku'aḥ nefesh* (permitting all activity in life-and-death emergencies) to all services deemed vital to the state's security, which presumably is the principle that is presently utilized.

Although these approaches are rooted in valid precedent, it is most unlikely that, given Israel's fractious religious spectrum, there could be any agreement either on reestablishing a Sanhedrin or on issuing *takkanot*. This is particularly the case with the increased power that has accrued to the Orthodox political parties from the 1988 elections. The Orthodox cannot even legislate for each other without arousing conflict; some Orthodox communities will not accept the kashrut certifications issued by other Orthodox rabbis who are not of their group.

The 1988 election results have serious implications for Israel's non-Orthodox and "secular" Jews. There surely will be further attempts to deny the Law of Return to non-Orthodox conversions, further restrictions on non-Orthodox services and rituals, and increased attacks on the legitimacy of Conservative Judaism.

In response, we must remember that our legitimacy is not dependent upon the recognition of Israeli Orthodox authorities. Therefore, we should be vigilant in insisting upon our rights and resisting, within the law, every threat to our status.

The maxim, "whom the gods would destroy they first make drunk with power," may well pertain to the present situation. The

Orthodox parties probably will overreach themselves and bring about a backlash. Despite our being a minority, we can, with forthright philosophical opposition, clearly demonstrate our approach to halakhah.

If we want to be a force in Israel today we must begin by providing leadership to our own group; to do otherwise is to become irrelevant. If we respect halakhah, we must muster the courage to apply the principle to guide Masorti Jews and even to influence others.

We should be committed to the eventual implementation of those portions of *Emet V'Emunah* (the Statement of Principles of Conservative Judaism) which call for greater separation of religion and the state in Israel. In practice, this means that (1) the laws of the State should not be used to support a single religious view or group; (2) the recognition of diversity of belief and religious practice; and (3) civil options for marriage and divorce for those who so prefer, while empowering each religious community to handle its own ritual requirements.[2]

Several implications follow from the above premises:

1. We should address ourselves to the implications of a Jewish State, and its functional corollary, the Law of Return, for both Judaism's and Israel's well-being.

2. We should oppose the contemporary rabbinic practice of utilizing a hotel's need for kashrut certification as leverage for prohibiting non-food functions, such as mixed swimming, New Year's Eve celebrations, and the use of elevators and microphones during the Sabbath.

Let there be an end to legislation by legal fiction. If a law is so outmoded that it is not observed, it should be set aside respectfully and without hypocrisy. Even biblical laws have been thus suspended (e.g., the laws of sacrifice). *Takkanot* (proclamations which modify Jewish Law), which are not without halakhic precedent, have guided the Conservative movement.

Traditionally, the State of Israel has been the fulfillment of a promise and the promise of even greater fulfillment. Without it our future would be painfully bleak. With Israel, the Jew has returned to the arena of political history, from which he has been absent for many centuries; without it, his or her future is in doubt.

However one defines Judaism, it clearly includes a religious faith, even though many Israelis practice no faith, yet insist that they are Jews. Furthermore, Jews do not comprise a nation, for they are citizens of many countries.

We Jews, then, are not and never have been a nation like other nations, or a religion like other religions.

In ancient times, we were a *goy kadosh* (holy people), a concept that does not translate well in a political dictionary. Today, there is an entity called the State of Israel. Is it a Jewish state or a state of the Jews? Or is it something else, an Israeli state?

During the period of our absence from political history, there were many states in which Jews lived, but in each of them they were outsiders. To be French was to be Catholic, to be English was to be Anglican, and to be Russian was to be Russian Orthodox, while to be Moroccan or Tunisian meant to be Moslem. Jews who lived in those countries were outsiders.

The French Revolution engendered a significant change in the definition of nations and nationalities, of states and citizenship. We Jews had no state. We became citizens of the state where we lived. Yet while we were "let in" in principle, in reality we were kept out or made to feel left out. Therefore, Zionism was born.

From Zion came the State of Israel: new wine in an old vessel. To apply the pre- and post-Emancipation idea of a religious polity to a modern post–World War II state is to preserve an anachronism. There are no Christian states in the world today, except for the semi-state called the Vatican. The Muslim states that do exist, as in Iran, only prove the anachronistic nature of a state defined by religion.

Just as the Jew was an outsider in a Christian state, so are Christian or Muslim citizens of Israel outsiders in the Jewish state. But since both Christians and Moslems are equal citizens, one cannot view Israel as a Jewish state.

Israel is a modern state that belongs to all its citizens, most, but not all, of whom are Jewish. Although "Jewish state" describes a socioreligious population rather than a political entity, the term is open to misinterpretation and does not reflect the legal status of either Christian or Moslem citizens of Israel. Thus, we should avoid its use.

What is the relationship of the American Jews to the State of Israel? The uniqueness and significance of Israel lies in its being the only state in the world with a Jewish majority and where Jewish values, ideals, and concepts, together with the Hebrew language, defines its culture. Its Sabbath is the seventh day, not the first, its national holidays are the Jewish festivals, and even in secular schools, the Bible and rabbinic literature are taught and Jewish observances acknowledged, even by non-Jewish citizens. The state is heir of the Jewish heritage's grandeur. Moreover, while Israel remains as Jewish as America is Christian, it need not be as Jewish as America is American.

As the concept of a Jewish state is dated and counterproductive, so too are the provisions of the Law of Return. Some suggest that our response to efforts to amend the law to recognize only converts "according to halakhah" should be to endorse this change—while insisting that, since our conversions follow halakhic procedures, our converts should be accorded recognition.

This approach ignores the fact that the Conservative Movement's unequivocal commitment to kashrut did not prevent the cancellation of our youth hostel's kashrut certificate. It subsequently was restored because the authorities realized that its denial could not be justified, and not because they suddenly had discovered our conformity to the halakhah. Because of Conservative theology, no change in ritual procedure will make us acceptable to Israel's Orthodox leaders.

Instead of encouraging aliyah, the Law of Return only encourages strife. According non-Jewish members of the Knesset the right to define Jewish identity "for the purpose of the Law of Return" is ludicrous and harmful because of the needless controversy it has aroused between Orthodox and non-Orthodox Israeli Jews.

The Law of Return was indispensable in providing the State of Israel with a Jewish majority. While there were Jews in displaced persons' camps, Jews without passports, Jews who lived as noncitizens in Muslim states, the Law of Return was essential for rescue and resettlement.

There are almost no Jewish displaced persons in camps. Any Jew in the free world can reach Israel without the Law of Return;

Jews in totalitarian countries may enter once they escape from their repressive borders. Normal immigration procedures could lead to citizenship for both groups without discrimination against non-Jews. Special attention and encouragement of Jewish settlement should be, and is, the province of the World Zionist Organization, not of the state.

The Law of Return presently is an irritant among various Jews and between Jews and non-Jews.[3]

The self-styled "nonviolent" Arab activist Mubarak Awad is neither a pacifist nor a fool. Upon being deported, he threatened to return to Israel by converting to Judaism and using his rights under the Law of Return. Yet however implausible the procedure, his strategy made for convincing propaganda. Other Arabs, who reside in Israel proper or the West Bank, complain that while they cannot become Israeli citizens, Ethiopian or Russian Jewish newcomers become instant citizens. Israeli and Diaspora Jewry alike are harmed by such negative propaganda.

Rather than oppose changing the Law of Return, then, we should seek to have it repealed.

4. To strengthen our position, we should collaborate more with the Reform Movement. For too long among Conservative Jews, anti-Reformism was a substitute for an ideology. In this, our second century, we should have the security to collaborate without fear of loss of identity.

Israel's Reform rabbinate also separates itself from those American Reform practices of which we disapprove, particularly patrilineal descent and condoning rabbis who participate in mixed marriages.

Our challengers on the Right reject both of us. If they divide us, they will prevail. Conversely, neither movement will succeed in Israel without the other. In fact, only because of our collaboration have we successfully withstood attempts to change the Law of Return.

In Israel, both movements are victims of a militant, intolerant, and fanatic minority which exercises a disproportionate influence over the personal lives of its citizens. It confuses compulsion with religion, and, conversely, pluralism with assimilation; it views alternative choices as immoral.

We should fight for a different Israel, one which is a democratic state serving citizens of diverse faiths and cultures, a refuge for Jews fleeing oppression, a welcome home for those who elect aliyah, and a creative repository of Judaism's values. In such an atmosphere, Conservative Judaism will flourish.

NOTES

1. Julien Weill, *Zadoc Kahn* (Paris: Librairie Felix Alcan, 1912), pp. 192–93. Quoted in S. Z. Abramov, *Perpetual Dilemma* (New York: World Union for Progressive Judaism, 1973), p. 65.

2. *Emet Ve'emunah,* New York, 1988, pp. 34–35.

3. It also is confusing: many metropolitan papers have stated incorrectly that the purpose of the Orthodox attempts to change the Law of Return is to deny Israeli citizenship to non-Orthodox converts. This ignores the fact that all Christian and Muslim immigrants to Israel have the right to apply for citizenship. The denial applies only to the immediate citizenship rights under the Law of Return, which the Orthodox would deny those who have converted to Judaism under Conservative or Reform auspices. The real intent of the attempt to change the law is not so much to deny rights of the convert but to deny the legitimacy of the officiating rabbi.

SEMINAR 4
Aliyah

What should the normative place of aliyah be in the Conservative Jewish consciousness? More practically, how should aliyah be presented to Conservative Jews?

At various times, leaders of our movement have articulated in practice, if not in so many words, at least three positions: (1) aliyah is the ultimate fulfillment of a life committed to Judaism and is, therefore, a step worthy of the strongest encouragement; (2) aliyah is one of many significant actions a Jew can take, but in promoting aliyah we have to adapt to the realistic conditions and priorities of life in the Diaspora; (3) not every Jew should make aliyah, but every (Conservative) Jew should ideally come to understand the personal challenge and opportunity offered by living in the Jewish State.

The issue here is not merely normative, but practical as well. How much effort should we indeed invest in the difficult task of promoting aliyah? What sorts of positive and negative side-effects do such efforts entail?

Aliyah: Abroad Thoughts from Home

JAC FRIEDGUT

I.

In characterizing Jewish migration to Israel as aliyah, we clearly make a value judgment that one is ascending, at least spiritually. For purposes of analyzing the existing situation, however, it is instructive to look at aliyah as migration, pure and simple.

One could devise a scale where countries would be placed according to whether they are "attracters" or "repellers." Among the former (which, because they attract immigrants, have legislation to keep them *out*) are the United States, Canada, and Australia. Among the repellers (which, because people seek to leave them, make special efforts to keep people *in*) are the Soviet Union, South Africa (for whites), Iran (for Jews), and certain South American countries.

Having migrated from a repeller (South Africa) to an attracter (United States), and subsequently emigrated again, I have given much thought to what makes an attracter attract. There seem to be two basic factors: the perception of unlimited or rapidly growing economic opportunities, and the perception of an open society that is free, and, *in practice,* not averse to accepting outsiders. Thus, in an attracter country, a newcomer is not perceived of as coming at the expense of the natives, and an ever-growing "pie" makes room for everyone. Economically, it is not a zero-sum game.

Where does Israel fit on this scale? The current controversy over direct flights for Soviet Jewish emigrants and the high rate of *noshrim* (drop-outs) among them are well-known phenomena. To take the other major repeller society, South African Jews, after coming to Israel in the first two decades following Israel's independence, recently have opted for the United States, Great Britain, Canada, or Australia in great numbers. Israelis themselves have been making *yeridah* not only to such attracters as the United States and Canada, but also to such repellers (for Jews) as West Germany and South Africa. This has occurred despite Israel's being the one country in the world that gives Jews a virtually automatic right to immigrate, and that even "pays them" to do so, via legislated benefits not available to Israel's other residents.[1]

I am an economist by training. I know that if one cannot manage financially, nothing else matters, as the following real cases illustrate:

1. L. and S. came to Israel as newlyweds imbued with the Zionist dream. Each eventually secured a part-time teaching job, which was the best they could find. Less than two years later, they went back to the States, convinced that if they remained in Israel, they would not be able to afford a home or a car, not to mention the cost of supporting a child.
2. C. and M. came as a young couple with a small daughter. After working in the public sector for about a year, C. decided to start a public relations business, with two partners. The couple bought a home in one of the outlying suburbs. But the business could not sustain three partners, so C. and M. rented out their new home, and returned to the States to make some money.
3. R. and G. came after a year of marriage and had a baby a few months after arriving. With a master's in physics, R. expected to get a decent job in his field and work on his Ph.D. at night. However, after almost a year of searching and scraping by with part-time English teaching, he and G. packed up and returned to the United States.

Thanks to the good Lord, Citibank, and the New Rochelle real estate market, our family came to Israel with a financial cushion.

Still, the old joke about getting a small fortune in Israel by coming with a big one is all too true.

Financial difficulties are not the only deterring factor; each day, we confront threats to our security. These threats, and responses to them, evoke questions about the morality of actions by the state and its leaders. Settling in Israel also involves being away from family and friends, struggling in a new language, and constantly fretting about your and your children's adjustment to the new land.

II.

Yet, having lived in Israel for over five years, I feel that it is *the* place for living Jewishly most fully, in accordance with mitzvot and halakhah.

How paradoxical that in the Torah, the basis of the symbiosis between Am Yisrael and Eretz Yisrael (the people of Israel and the land of Israel), four-fifths of the text finds us Jews outside of the Land. Most of the time, we appear as a ragged grouping of tribes wandering around in a desert, on our way, but (at least through the end of the Torah) not quite getting there. The generation enslaved in Egypt, emancipated by God, brought into an eternal covenant at Sinai, and going to the border of the Promised Land, was the "base" for Israel the land and Israel the people.

I am someone who "went up" to Israel in his mid-forties. As a modern equivalent of the *dor ba-midbar* (generation of the desert), as is perhaps every *oleh* above a certain age, I will never speak Hebrew with the same facility that I speak English, and will never hold a position equivalent to what I had at Citibank. In general, I will not become an intrinsic part of the fabric of Israel society, nor will all my children do so. However, some of them will, as will their children and *their* children.

Rabbis have given countless *divrei Torah* (words of Torah) about the people's pledge at Sinai, *na'aseh ve-nishma'* ("we will do and we will hear"). We pledged to obey God's mitzvot, even while trying to fathom their rationale and meaning. Aliyah is the ultimate *na'aseh ve-nishma'*. Sometimes I wonder what I am doing in Israel, but here I am. My destiny and that of the generations following me are intertwined now with the corporate and holistic destiny of the Jewish people.

As a Conservative Jew, I also am helping build a necessary infrastructure for the movement in Israel: forty-some synagogues, Camp Ramah and other youth programs, Kibbutz Hanaton, and educational institutions from a rabbinic seminary to the Tali schools.

III.

What of the institutional challenges and dilemmas the challenge of aliyah poses for the Conservative Movement?

1. Part of America's great beauty and worth is that it is a pluralistic society in which different groups can observe Saturday (or Sunday) as their Sabbath with impunity, or practice various types of dietary restrictions. An active campaign for aliyah, which may be viewed as "abandoning" America, raises issues of great delicacy and sensitivity, particularly when American and Israeli interests seem less convergent than in the past.

2. One expects that a rabbi or other movement leader who preaches kashrut, Shabbat, or love of one's fellow human will practice what he or she preaches. But when it comes to aliyah, this simply is not the case (with such rare exceptions as Rabbi Shlomo Riskin).

3. In suggesting that there be a "categorical imperative" for aliyah, I am using a Kantian term to suggest that everyone should act in this way. If they did, the numbers involved would eventually acquire substantial dimensions. Some suggest that this might seriously weaken the movement in the United States.

These caveats should make us more circumspect with respect to both the theory and practice of aliyah, but should not deter us from adopting a pro-aliyah program.

IV.

When all is said and done, expanded aliyah by American Jews, particularly Conservative ones, is in our best interests.

To paraphrase what a wag once said about Washington, D.C.,

Israel combines the best of Western charm and hospitality with Eastern efficiency. Israel is much more Western in its aspirations than in its operational approach to realizing them. Western Jews' constributions can be precisely in those areas whose lack we most deplore: economics, particularly efficiency and streamlining, reward by merit rather than seniority, and some degree of a market economy with reduced governmental intervention, as well as in politics, particularly greater democracy and political accountability, tolerance, and pluralism.

Religious pluralism is important to us Western Jews. In America, we value the separation between church and state, although this clearly cannot simply be transplanted to Israel. However, the Jewishness which should suffuse the Jewish State must permit a variety of hues reflecting the honest, intellectually grounded differences among us on the nature of halakhah.

Economic, social, and religious transformations will not come about on their own. Israel is caught in a "Catch-22": It is unlikely that there will be mass aliyah from the West until the socioeconomic fabric and *structure* of religion are more Western, but these changes probably will not take place until more Western, religiously tolerant Jews live in Israel as citizens and voters. One of the greatest challenges facing the Conservative Movement, in devising an effective aliyah policy, is breaking this "Catch-22."

On the basis of the above point, we should adopt the following strategy:

1. The Conservative Movement should elevate aliyah to among the most crucial mitzvot, along with Shabbat and kashrut. We should express this commitment not by passing resolutions, but by a detailed, well-thought-out action program, initiated by the leadership of all the movement's arms.

2. The movement must raise substantial funds to foster aliyah among Conservative Jews, and to assist those already in Israel, via a free loan fund of up to $10 million by 1995. Doing this would provide significant tangible support to actual and prospective *olim,* and would send a much stronger message than scores of resolutions. It also would represent a revolutionary broadening of the Foundation for Masorti Judaism's goal of fostering Conservative

Jews, along with Conservative Jewish institutions and staff, in Israel.

3. We should give special attention to education, particularly the Tali (strengthening Jewish studies) track in government schools. Such programs not only serve Conservative *olim,* but also can attract native Israelis to a philosophy of "enlightened Jewish living."

4. We should deploy significant resources to supporting *olim* in Israel, particularly through working closely with and strengthening the Association of Americans and Canadians in Israel, and through supporting religious pluralism and other Conservative objectives. American Conservative and Israeli Masorti Jews also should design and implement pilot trips for potential *olim.* They also should support the integration of *olim,* perhaps through a "buddy" system between each *oleh* and a family that has lived in Israel for some time.

5. We should strengthen such programs as Ramah, USY, junior year in Israel, and internships in Israel, for they have demonstrated success in "producing" (and preparing) future *olim.*

6. Mercaz might expand its role to establish regional and synagogue-based *ḥugei ivrit* (Hebrew study circles). It also should sponsor such practical pre-aliyah activities as pilot trips to Israel, vocational counseling for future *olim,* and assistance with housing and shipping personal property there. However, Mercaz must not be Conservative Judaism's only locus for Zionist activities or a "dumping ground" for aliyah, which *must* be a top priority for the entire movement.

7. One cannot *cause* aliyah by setting numerical targets. However, the Conservative Movement's leadership should look to the basic organizational unit of Conservative Jews—the synagogue—to foster aliyah. It should be an attainable goal that one family (plus a few singles) each year go on aliyah from small and medium-sized synagogues, with perhaps two or three times that amount from larger synagogues.

If we will it—and have the courage to set an example—aliyah is no dream.

Aliyah

SYNOPSIS

To understand why aliyah has not "caught fire" among American Jews, we should consider the general factors motivating emigration from repeller countries and immigration to attracters.

For people from the United States, moving to Israel seems to go against the grain because of—

- the perception of limited economic opportunities, and doubts about "making it";
- the perception of a society less free and open than America's;
- a host of other problems, ranging from security to the difficulty of finding a new professional and/or personal niche.

Nevertheless, for committed Jews, Israel is the only place where one can live one's Jewish commitment to the fullest. However, we must realize that olim above a certain age may feel like the *dor bamidbar* in Israel. But their destiny—and that of the generations following—will be intertwined with Am Yisrael in Eretz Yisrael.

Despite the difficulty of making aliyah for American Jews, we cannot afford *not* to espouse aliyah and not to design a strong and effective program to foster it among our members in an active way. The major elements in such a program should include:

1. Without fanfare and resolutions, but quietly and firmly, the movement's leadership (including all branches) should include aliyah among the most crucial mitzvot, along with Shabbat and kashrut.
2. The Foundation for Masorti Judaism must radically broaden its purposes, and raise significant additional funds to establish a sizeable loan fund for Conservative *olim*.
3. We should support such aliyah-strengthening programs as the Tali schools, Ramah, USY in Israel, junior year abroad, and internship programs in Israel.
4. The movement in Israel should constitute a support system for new *olim*.
5. Mercaz should become particularly active in promoting and

practically supporting aliyah, which must, however, be a movement-wide concern.

6. Each synagogue should strive to generate *olim* from among its membership.

NOTE

1. Two brief comments on these benefits: first, every concession the Israeli government makes to *olim* (new immigrants) at the expense of others engenders a certain resentment, particularly when the *olim* emigrate from the "affluent West." Second, prospective immigrants who choose a country on the basis of economic factors would much rather opt for one with more opportunities, less regulation, and a sympathetic or neutral tax system, as opposed to Israel's current economic system. Thus, the very socioeconomic system that grants the *oleh* concessions is inimical to what he is seeking.

Aliyah and Alternatives to Aliyah

PAULA HYMAN

It may be that flourishing mundanely in the civility and security of South Orange, more or less forgetful from one day to the next of your Jewish origins but remaining identifiably (and voluntarily) a Jew, you were making Jewish history no less astonishing than theirs, though without quite knowing it every moment, and without having to say it.—Philip Roth, *The Counterlife*

All contemporary Jews who take their Jewishness seriously must confront the opportunity and challenge presented by the State of Israel. After almost two millennia of exile, Jews have returned to Zion and are struggling to build and sustain a society that will meet its citizens' needs while providing fertile ground for the flourishing of Jewish culture. The future of world Jewry and of Judaism depends upon the outcome of that struggle.

Zionism has "conquered the [Jewish] communities" to an extent unimaginable at the beginning of this century. However, it has not inspired the masses of Jews living in the West to commit their lives to building a Jewish society in a remote and comparatively poor corner of the world. For Israelis, the failure of aliyah remains a painful subject. At numerous meetings of Diaspora and Israeli leaders, we are told that mass aliyah from the West can provide the demographic guarantee of Israel's security and commitment to the Western values of democracy and pluralism. Conservative Jews in Israel have argued that a substantial aliyah of their American counterparts will enable the Masorti Movement to become more firmly established and to secure the societal and governmental recognition to which it is entitled.

There is every reason for the Conservative Movement to present aliyah as an exciting and meaningful way of contributing to Jewish history and deepening one's knowledge and experience of Judaism. But the movement should refrain from portraying aliyah as "the ultimate fulfillment of a life committed to Judaism."

When we suggest that aliyah is the fulfillment of commitment to Judaism, we make a number of implicit assumptions that contradict our history and experience. We deny the possibility of continuing Jewish creativity and vitality, including spiritual vitality, in the Diaspora. We also suggest that a life of Jewish commitment in the Diaspora necessarily must be not only different from life in the Jewish state, but also Jewishly inferior.

Yet despite Eretz Yisrael's centrality in Jewish thought, rabbinic Judaism is by-and-large a product of the Diaspora. The development of Conservative Judaism, in particular, is intimately linked with American values. Many of us believe that the interaction of Judaism with different cultures has been, and can continue to be, fruitful. On a personal level, we feel that, whatever the vacuousness of much of American Jewish life, there are here spiritually rich Jewish communities of great potential.

Our efforts to live a Judaism rooted in tradition, yet infused by the best values of Western modernity, have been nurtured particularly by the pluralism of American society—a pluralism which is notably, and unfortunately, absent in Israel. We who have spent time in Israel have come to realize that our possibilities for Jewish religious expression are actually broader in America than in Israel. Here, we must contend with the forces of assimilation, indifference, and ignorance, but not with forces that reject Western modernity or with the power of a governmentally-recognized religious establishment. This establishment denies the legitimacy of, and attempts to repress, the very expression of our Judaism.

In promoting aliyah, we would inadvertently follow the same path as those who define Conservative Judaism as a concession to weakness. From this perspective, Conservative Jews are simply lapsed Orthodox Jews unable to accept the discipline of halakhah, while Diaspora Jews are simply failed Zionists unable to forgo creature comforts. This approach, which denies the validity of our community, our reading of Jewish history, and our religious movement, is counter-productive. Jews do not make a decision for aliyah on the basis of guilt or self-deprecation, nor do they engage in fruitful Israel-Diaspora dialogue when one partner sees the other primarily in terms of demographic renewal.

How, then, do we present aliyah to Conservative Jews? It must emerge as one of a number of life choices confronting Jews who are committed to Judaism and to Jewish survival. If the Conservative Movement succeeds in educating its members to appreciate deeply Judaism and Jewish culture, it inevitably will introduce them to Israel's accomplishments and to the challenges that the state poses. It is no accident that so many Conservative religious and educational professionals and their children have made aliyah during the past two decades. In its education about Israel, the movement should highlight the special contribution that Conservative Jews can make to Jewish culture in Israel, as well as the ways that Israel can expand the scope of their Jewishness. Aliyah thus might best be seen as a possible, and desirable, consequence of quality Conservative Jewish education—a welcome by-product, but not the central focus, of that education.

In practical terms, I recommend that the Conservative Movement avoid expending its scarce resources to directly promote aliyah. Such an investment would be ineffective and would duplicate the efforts of other institutions. Paradoxically, the best way to stimulate Conservative aliyah is to invest in comprehensive, not aliyah-focused, Jewish education in the Diaspora.

However, benign neglect of the subject of aliyah should not imply indifference to Israel or to Israeli culture. If we are to remain one people, more American Jews must develop a personal relationship with Israel and Israelis, a visceral tie that transcends tourism. Of course, Israeli Jews also should develop a more sophisticated understanding of American Jews. The Conservative Movement might encourage its members to forge personal connections with Israel that go beyond political and financial support.

Educational programs such as Nativ, the Ramah Seminar in Israel and Midreshet Yerushalayim, which offer Jewish youth a serious introduction to Israel and Jewish study, should be expanded and promoted more vigorously. Study and intensive travel in Israel have proved effective as way-stations on the road towards aliyah. Just as some Conservative congregations have offered membership discounts to congregants who enroll their children in Solomon Schechter day schools, so synagogues might establish scholarship funds to defray the cost of Conservative programs in Israel. American Orthodox day schools have made postgraduation study in Israel virtually *de rigueur*. Likewise, Solomon Schechter day schools, USY, and Conservative high school programs could promote study in Israel, or living on Kibbutz Hanaton, as the culmination of a serious Jewish curriculum.

Incorporating Israel into the lives of American Jewish adults is more difficult. Most do not see aliyah as desirable; the few who do are constrained by family considerations, career demands, or love of America and contentment with its familiar environment. However, it is possible that American Jews could be inspired to enhance their involvement with Israel through "sojourning." By this, I mean periodic extended visits to Israel to experience its society and day-to-day routine, and to create bonds with the land and its people. The academic sabbatical provides an obvious model for such sojourning. But even those not blessed with the freedom of an academic calendar might consider committing vacation time to volunteer work or adult education programs in Israel. Such sojourns will strengthen Jewish identity and commitment even in the absence of aliyah and will heighten the prospects for meaningful dialogue between American and Israeli Jews.

To strengthen Conservative Jews' attachment to Israel, the movement also should reemphasize its commitment to Hebrew as both the language of our classic texts and the language of contemporary Israeli culture. Too often, our teaching of Hebrew is limited to preparing individuals to read the *siddur*. The excitement of Hebrew' rebirth as a language of daily life and cultural creativity—an excitement that was palpable only a generation ago—has been lost. Were a substantial number of American Jews to share a Jewish language with their Israeli counterparts, we would lay the foundations for mutual respect, for a joint exploration of those issues which bind us together even under vastly different circumstances.

I have deliberately strayed from the topic of aliyah as narrowly defined because for the committed American Jew, aliyah is only one response, and not the most accessible, to the reality of Israel. The Conservative Movement has an obligation to instill in its members with love of Israel, its land and its people. Focusing on aliyah, however, is neither the most practical way to achieve that goal, nor the approach most consonant with either our sense of history or our self-definition.

The Conservative Movement recognizes and encourages aliyah as a significant response to the challenges offered by the existence of the State of Israel. Yet it also recognizes the viability and ongoing creativity of the America Diaspora in which it has been nurtured.

The movement should be committed to educating its members about the significance of Israel and to deepening their visceral attachment to the land and its people. While aliyah would be a welcome by-product of an intensive Conservative Jewish education, serious attention to Israel will derive from this approach:

1. Promotion and expansion of Conservative programs of study and living in Israel appropriate to different age groups; increased involvement of congregations in supporting such programs and recruiting participants.

2. Encouragement of "sojourning" visits to Israel, perhaps with ties to Masorti institutions.

3. Exploration of ways to foster the learning of Hebrew as an essential affective and practical link with Israel.

SUMMARY

The Conservative Movement recognizes, and encourages, aliyah as a significant response to the challenges offered by the existence of the State of Israel. Yet it also acknowledges the viability and ongoing creativity of the American Diaspora in which it has been nurtured.

The movement has a commitment to educate its members as to the significance of Israel and to deepen their visceral attachment to the land and its people. Aliyah would be a welcome by-product of an intensive Conservative Jewish education, serious attention to

Israel and its meaning as a component of the movement's educational and cultural programming is an important end in itself.

Several proposals aimed at enhancing personal connection with Israel emerge from this approach:

1) Promotion and expansion of Conservative programs of study and living in Israel appropriate to different age groups. Increased involvement of congregations in supporting such programs and recruiting participants.
2) Encouragement of "sojourning" visits to Israel, perhaps with ties to Masorti institutions.
3) Exploration of ways to foster the learning of Hebrew as an essential effective and practical link with Israel.

North American Conservative Judaism and Education

BENJAMIN J. SEGAL

I believe that special efforts should be made by American Jewish educators to encourage their pupils to think of the possibility of *aliyah*, but these efforts must center upon positive rather than negative factors . . . developing a commitment . . . which will see in life in Israel a unique opportunity for spiritual self-fulfillment as an individual and as a Jew.
—Simon Greenberg[1]

The fighting edge of Zionism must be our emphasis on *aliyah* as the foremost Zionist *mitzvah*, our stress on the kind of Zionist education which will predispose Jewish youngsters to making *aliyah*.
—Israel Goldstein[2]

Aliyah ("ascent") means more than moving to Israel—it indicates emigrating there for reasons of one's Jewishness, moving to gain advantages not available elsewhere. However, it does not presume *shilat ha-golah* (the negation of the Diaspora). In fact, experience tells us that the opposite is true—that aliyah is an outgrowth of Jewish commitment in the Golah (Diaspora).

Most aliyah from North America is a result of intensive Jewish involvement in the Diaspora, followed by the conclusion that Israel can offer an added dimension to an individual's life that the Diaspora cannot.[3] Aliyah, then, is a *further* stage in Jewish growth that seeks depth, breadth, or public support for private commitments.

Emphasis on aliyah is not antithetical to other aspects of Jewish education; indeed it can be supportive thereof. If there are several ways to "ascend" to the top floor, all necessarily involve progress by steps; certainly, one can never ascend by denying the ground on which one stands. We therefore reject that approach to aliyah education which is confrontational, assuming the imminent or eventual dissolution of the Galut.[4] Israel, then, is seen as the necessary component of greatest Jewish fulfillment, and emphasis falls within the framework of encouragement of all other aspects of Jewish observance and commitment.

The opposite of such "aliyah inclination" would be a basic satisfaction with the actual and potential Diaspora environment. An approach which finds Jewish life in the Diaspora potentially as fulfilling as in Israel *ipso facto* will not encourage aliyah, which presupposes unique benefits from living in Israel. These include "new horizons," such as ease of observance, the Hebrew language, and a national culture base.[5]

ALIYAH AND EDUCATION

The educational program I propose is inclusive and supportive of aliyah.[6] What follows are analyses of the Jewish educational framework, three aspects of content (the reality of Israel versus myth, emphasizing differences from the Diaspora as opposed to similarities, and direct reference to aliyah), the appropriate formats for such education, and the appropriate age at which students might be instructed therein.

1. *The Jewish educational framework.* Jewish education should not restrict itself to immediately "relevant" items, nor to material easily achievable in the Diaspora. Specifically, spoken Hebrew, aspects of Jewish culture (e.g., art, dance, and drama), and communal celebrations should be encouraged with both appreciation for students' achievements and acknowledgment of the inherent limitations of the Diaspora environment. The implied Zionist message is that Jewish culture is more easily achieved in Israel.

Second, time spent in Israel must be part of the educational "ladder" which one climbs. The more one visits Israel and, specifically, the longer one stays as a teenager, the greater the chance of aliyah.

2. *Content: Emphasize the reality, not the myth.* To encourage aliyah, teaching of Israel should communicate the reality of Israel, a task complicated by fundraising efforts which emphasize the myths of heroism, poverty, and nostalgia (Israel as "instant old country"), as well as distortions inherent to the tradition's messianism.[7]

Many educational programs in the Diaspora and Israel itself encourage old myths concerning Israel and build new ones. These myths have developed as a natural defense against the demand to make aliyah (from a time, admittedly, when that act was far more difficult than it is today). A few programs, however, have successfully demonstrated that one can emphasize the country's difficult, complex reality.[8]

But does one not make aliyah precisely for the dream of Israel? In the past, the myth of Israel was its principal attraction, reflecting past or future glory. Today, the real Israel must be presented as an alternative to Diaspora life, as a country that provides greater depth, breadth, and public support for the world-view of Conservative Judaism. Thus, myths should not be necessary to attract aliyah.

Furthermore, the myths, being largely false, undermine the process of *kelitah* (absorption). There are inevitably difficult adjustments within the *kelitah* process. We need not further "stack the deck" against the *oleh* through easily shatterable myths.

There is an interesting correspondence between travel to Israel and "myth-breaking." Evidence shows that those who have been to Israel more have a more negative image of the country, but closer connection to it.[9] The true image of Israel does not drive Jews away from it.

This emphasis on the real Israel reflects the Conservative Jewish stance, whereby Jewish value concepts correspond to contemporary realities. Unless the value concept "Eretz Yisrael" is inclusive of the state's present reality, it loses its relevance.

3. *Emphasize differences, not similarities.* Most North American Jewish textbooks about Israel gloss over the major differences between Jewish life there and in the Diaspora. There exist such

implicit and explicit parallels as: we are all democratic, we all care for the poor, and we are all descended from pioneers.[10] This distortion bears the message: the values we express can be achieved equally well here or there.

Aliyah-inclusive Jewish education must emphasize the differences between Israel and Diaspora, in kind and in degree. It is precisely these differences which will lead to personal confrontation with the challenge of aliyah; an Israel which is similar does not do so.

Surprisingly, even many programs in Israel encourage Diaspora Jewish life. They often emphasize such areas as ritual observance, synagogue life, and tzedakah (charity). Those subjects are best taught in schools, homes, camps, and youth movements, while Israel visits should be used to teach the country's distinctiveness as a Jewish environment.

Within this framework, there are three different formats which are based on successful youth movement or organizational programs in Israel:

1. Concentration on challenges available to Jews only in Israel (e.g., the ethics of war, building Jerusalem, or national culture).[11]
2. Focus on *potential* reality—what the country could be if members of that movement contributed their unique expertise and world-view.[12]
3. Using historical models to relate to Israel—a nonthreatening confrontation with the subject.[13]

4. *Directly confront aliyah*. While aliyah sits atop a continuum of Jewish experience, concentration on these other aspects rarely leads to a confrontation with the question of aliyah. We must therefore reject the view that the best way to encourage aliyah is simply to teach Jewishness; rather, aliyah must be structured into the educational system.[14]

In presenting aliyah, curricular planners must reflect the interaction among the subject, the students, the teachers, and the community. These considerations lead to the following emphases:

1. We approach aliyah as an option, privilege, and opportunity, as opposed to an obligation. Thus the term mitzvah would be appropriate only in its Yiddish sense of a good act, and not in its Hebrew sense of a requirement.
2. In speaking of obligation, we refer to considering and deciding about, as opposed to making, aliyah.
3. In using value judgments, we should use those of degree rather than polarized absolutes (e.g., not good-bad or true-false, but more fulfilling—less fulfilling).
4. We emphasize the attraction of Israel, not flight from the Diaspora.

However, premature or overly confrontational consideration of aliyah is counterproductive. Presenting various historical models of relating to Israel, including aliyah, probably represents a better approach.[15]

5. *Formats.* There is little room within the formal Jewish educational world for progress in presenting aliyah given the nature of the faculties, time limitations, and the tendency toward "relevance" in developing high school subjects so as to attract the most students. Development of aliyah-oriented curricula should be designed primarily for formal aspects of relatively informal programs (e.g., trips to Israel, camping, and youth group discussions).[16]

6. *Age.* Evidence indicates that basic changes in personal orientation occur most often during the college years, particularly through the influence of environment as opposed to formal education.[17] Unfortunately, Jewish educational networks, including those of the Conservative Movement, have little contact with students during those years, although relatively large numbers attend college-year programs in Israel. We should carefully consider how to encourage such formal and informal education, and how to deepen the confrontation with aliyah in Israel or other "total environments."

PRACTICAL SUGGESTIONS FOR THE CONSERVATIVE MOVEMENT

The Jewish Theological Seminary of America should strictly apply the requirement that rabbinical students spend a year in Israel.

Moreover, the timing should be changed to the penultimate year of study, when students are more knowledgeable, and more able to appreciate the state (the present requirement uses Israel as a training ground for basic skills). The curriculum within Israel should be more Israel-focused in terms of history and Zionist ideology.

Mercaz, with United Synagogue, should create Israel committees in each synagogue. Such committees would encourage the celebration of Yom ha-Atzma'ut (Israel Independence Day), organize Israel trips, and celebrate together with the congregation any congregant's forthcoming aliyah. This framework should be used to encourage participation in the existing network of the movement's Israel activities, as well as a student's spending a college year in Israel (ideally, through the Seminary's program, Midreshet Yerushalayim).

USY and Ramah should provide more opportunities for a study on Israel and enhance the Israel emphasis of programs there. Zionist intervention on campuses, particularly in Israel, should be expanded.

The Solomon Schechter Schools should establish an eighth-grade trip to Israel as the experience of the school, and as a spur to subsequent trips. Key new elements of the curriculum might prepare students for such a trip.

Conservative rabbis should abandon the tour model for study visits to Israel, working instead through Mercaz, the Masorti Foundation, and the Ramah Israel Institute.

Congregational programming should include an annual Israel visit regardless of the number participating. The congregation should commit the rabbi's time for this, preceded by preparatory courses.

Congregants also should have direct contact with Conservative *olim* (both in Israel and as guest speakers at the synagogue).

Among other steps the Conservative Movement can take in support of aliyah are to provide extensive information on Israeli life in movement and synagogue publications, to recognize *olim* and to help them with financial assistance (e.g., interest-free loans).

NOTES

1. Simon Greenberg, "The Role of Israel in American Jewish Education," *Jewish Education* 42, nos. 2–3 (Spring 1973): 32 f.
2. Speech, April 1968, to Jerusalem Journalists Association, cited in Israel Goldstein, *Jewish Perspectives* (Jerusalem: Keter, 1985), p. 258.
3. See Kevin Avruch, *American Immigrants in Israel* (Chicago: University of Chicago Press, 1981).
4. E.g., A. B. Yehoshua, "The Golah as a Neurotic Solution," *Forum*, Spring–Summer 1979, pp.34 f. "Instead of engaging in Jewish education in the Golah, we must engage exclusively in the promotion of *aliya*."
5. Some Conservative circles may see Diaspora life as truly fulfilling. The challenge facing us is to expand such individuals' horizons so as to include such advantages as those noted here.
6. These comments reflect to some extent discussions and reports at a seminar I conducted at the Melton Center of the Hebrew University in 1987–88. I wish to acknowledge the contributions of the seminar's participants.
7. Harold I. Greenberg, "The UJA's Israel: Implications for American Aliyah," *Forum*, Fall–Winter 1979, pp. 109–114.
8. See Benjamin Segal, " 'Israel' vs. 'Zionist' Education: The Summer Trip Model," *Jewish Education* 55, no. 3 (Fall 1989): 30–36.
9. Steven M. Cohen, *Jewish Travel to Israel* (Jerusalem: Jewish Agency and Jewish Education Committee, 1986) pp. 14 f.
10. David Breakstone, *"The Dynamics of Israel in American Jewish Life: An Analysis of Educational Means as Cultural Texts"* (Ph.D. diss., Hebrew University, 1987), p. 131.
11. An example is the program of the Ramah Seminar in Israel; see Segal, op. cit.
12. This was the model pursued across the years by some of the Zionist movement's year courses in Israel.
13. This would be a variation of the High School in Israel program, which is based on historical examples, but does not specifically use models of association with Israel. Their model would have to be combined with study of material such as that in my *Returning* (see below).
14. Cf. Yitzhak Rabin, "Israel and American Jews," *Forum*, Spring 1975, pp. 68–74.
15. History provides a range of relationships to Israel which are fascinating, and which can be used as comparisons to our present relationships. See Benjamin Segal, *Returning: The Land of Israel as a Focus in Jewish History* (Jerusalem: World Zionist Organization, 1987), and Eliezer Schweid, *Moledet ve-Eretz Ye'udah* [Homeland and a Land of Promise] (Tel Aviv; Am Oved, 1979), now available in an English version through Herzl Press, New York.
16. The series *Viewpoints*, published by the American Association for Jewish Education (now JESNA), New York, 1973, is particularly informative. Unfortunately, this material has not been updated, but it is still in large part usable, particularly the pamphlet on aliyah by Yigael Bruckenstein [Barkan].
17. For an early indication, see Philip E. Jacob, *Changing Values in College* (New York: Harper & Bros., 1957).

Eretz Yisrael and Aliyah: A Jewish Zionist View

JOSEPH S. WERNIK

Now that the Conservative Movement has become an integral part of the World Zionist Organization, we should closely examine our understanding of, and commitment to, Zionism and aliyah. Although some individuals have made aliyah, there has been no systematic or coordinated movement program to encourage immigration to Israel.

Traditional and modern sources point to aliyah as an existential need for the Jewish people, the individual, Conservative Judaism, and the State of Israel.

Each Jew's religious imperative to reside in Israel is expressed in one of the Torah's basic commands: "And you shall dwell in the land which I have given unto your ancestors; and ye shall be my people and I will be unto you your God," and in the *Ketuvim:* "For God will deliver Zion, and the cities of Judah will be rebuilt wherein they will dwell and inherit it [the Land]."

The most eminent of our legal interpreters have shown that this supreme religious imperative operates in our own times. The Ramban clearly indicates in his addenda to *Sefer ha-Mitzvot* (mitzvah 4) of Maimonides: "Since this mitzvah [of aliyah] operates timelessly, each Jew, even the one who has made the Golah his home, must at all times strive to make this imperative a tangible reality in his own life." There is a story in the Sifrei (*Parshat Re'eh*, piska 8) that relates how the rabbis wept as they remembered Israel when they were far away, and immediately decided to return to their homeland. This story served as proof that "dwelling in Eretz Yisrael is equated with all the Torah precepts put together." And the Ramban, in his commentary to the Torah (the end of *Aharei Mot*), stipulates "that the fundamental aim of all the Torah precepts is to see all of Israel dwelling in the land."

THE LAND AND THE PEOPLE

Professor Eliezer Schweid demonstrates the key role of Eretz Yisrael in Jewish life, using as prooftexts the Bible, the oral teachings, philosophical and kabbalistic thought, and modern Hebrew literature.[1] In ancient times, when the people dwelt in the land, there was a unique relationship between the land of national destiny as promised in the Torah and the actual homeland in which the people lived. Following the exile, the land remained in the people's memories and visions as a future land of destiny. Zionism, despite its impressive achievements, is still far from uniting these two "lands." Most Jews still look upon the land from the perspective of exile. We will confront today the same tension between the actual homeland and its symbolic destiny, as we attempt to realize the goals of Zionism. Therefore, we must form a bridge with the past, and rediscover the Jewish sources from which Zionism drew its driving force.

THE LAND THE THE INDIVIDUAL

Another Israeli philosopher, Alexander Barzel, states that the State of Israel is the only place wherein one can live a fulfilled Jewish life.[2] The life of the Jew is one of reception (what he has absorbed from the past) and transmission (what he hands down to future generations). A whole individual is one who creates harmony between his world-view and his daily existence. When he is prevented from institutionalizing his world-view, either by external pressure (as in the USSR) or by alienation and assimilation (as in the United States), he experiences an identity crisis. Zionism attempts to institutionalize the Jewish world-view of reception and transmission. Aliyah resolves the crisis of Jewish identity, since the State of Israel is the only framework in which one can realize the world-view from which flows his self-awareness of identity and thus live a completely fulfilled Jewish life.

Professor Ephraim Urbach states that aliyah presents a moral challenge.[3] The state created a framework within which the Jewish people's ideological differences and controversies can be confronted directly and openly. The success of Zionism, its impact on human civilization, depends on the number of Jews ready to meet this challenge. This involves preparation for aliyah, followed by actual emigration to Israel. At the least, it means encouraging Jews to view themselves as candidates for aliyah.

ALIYAH AND THE AMERICAN JEWISH COMMUNITY

Professor Arthur Hertzberg maintains that the leaders of American Zionism originally backed Zionism principally because they believed that the tie with Eretz Yisrael would lend new substance to Jewish life.[4] He contends that American Jewry is primarily involved in Israel's economic and political affairs, but not in Israeli culture. However, this kind of attachment to Israel does not really benefit the American Jewish community and will not stop the erosion of Jewish identity in America's open society. For the basic threat to American Jewry is not anti-Semitism, but assimilation. Professor Hertzberg maintains that mainstream American Jewry will survive only if it solves its internal, cultural-religious crisis of identity.

Lack of satisfaction with the Galut, and vital interest in Israel, necessitates revitalizing Jewish education. Hertzberg notes that one sign of American Zionism's weakness is its negligible influence: the lack of Zionist schools and teachers' seminars as important tools for shaping the character of American Jews. Were we to stress the importance of Jewish education and Jewish culture, we would perhaps be closer to the messianic redemption, "ingathering the exiles." He concludes that the first task facing Zionism in the Diaspora is to ensure that every Jewish child receives a Jewish-Zionist education and spends time in an organized program in Israel. Only thus will he be able to face the challenge of aliyah.

Professor Simon Halkin states that the attraction of the Jewish masses to the "good life" in the Galut means that aliyah initially will only be undertaken by a "relatively small number of individuals."[5] Were American Zionism to educate these "few," thousands of young American Jews ultimately might follow in their wake.

Rather than hearing how much Israel "needs him," a Jewish young person must come to the deep-seated realization of how much he needs Israel. After all, he is a Jew living in a non-Jewish society with a non-Jewish culture; he knows in his soul that there is no life more congenial to the Jewish psyche than in Eretz Yisrael. This "positive Zionism" must be inculcated into the individual from early childhood into adolescence and beyond.

ALIYAH: A NEED OF THE DIASPORA AND OF ISRAEL

Aliyah represents a mutual need of the Diaspora and of Israel. Professor Natan Rotenstreich observes that an influx of Western Jewry in Israel will open new horizons despite the tensions inherent in its existence.[6] But it would be a mistake for Zionists to use this argument in basing their call for aliyah. Rather, aliyah is for those Western Jews who prefer the struggle for the Jewish people's role in the world over the daily comforts of Diaspora existence because they realize that affluence is not sufficient to solve the problem of personal identity and meaning.

Arnold Eisen, professor of religious studies at Stanford University, has written eloquently along these lines concerning the challenge of aliyah:

> I regard the State of Israel as a great and terrible blessing. What does one do, as a Jew, in the face of such a blessing? At the very least, if Jewishness is at the center of one's life, one takes it with the ultimate personal seriousness. One asks, more than once, at more than one stage of life—whether one should not be living there. . . . One goes, if one so decides, because one physically cannot sit by and let other people blow it. The arrogance in the refusal to let others ruin things, while we sit idly by, is the arrogance necessary for "Tikkun Olam," our collective refusal as Jews to accept the world as it is. Humility in this regard could be fatal. . . . One is to rule out aliyah on the grounds

that the state is not worthy of us. . . . All the more reason to be there, where our dissatisfactions can at least lead to constructive protest. . . . Here [in America] we can never know if our self-righteousness is not fueled in part by guilt serving our rationalization. There [in Israel] we have the discomfort of finding that those with whom we disagree most profoundly are good neighbors, intelligent and committed. The good fight is to be fought there—with and against Israelis—not here. . . . I am only arguing that if we take seriously our responsibility to ask the question of Aliyah, we cannot let ourselves be dissuaded either by dissatisfaction with Israeli society or by our personal indispensability to American Jewish life.[7]

In his discussion on Israel as a factor in the American Jewish experience, *Beit Yisrael be-Amerika,* Professor Moshe Davis maintains that Eretz Yisrael is a source of life for Diaspora Jewish communities in general, and for American Jewry in particular; a Jewishly creative life is possible only in Israel. The duty of Diaspora communities is to ensure the State of Israel's future through fulfilling the command of Yishuv Eretz Yisrael (settling of Israel). This ultimate Jewish fulfillment is incumbent on every Diaspora Jew as a means of enriching the content of Jewish life. Also, aliyah enhances the Jewish character of Diaspora communities and so must be widely promoted within them.

DIRECTIONS FOR THE CONSERVATIVE MOVEMENT

How can the Conservative Movement educate toward aliyah and present it as an option for Jewish self-realization? I believe that ultimate Jewish fulfillment is found only through aliyah, and Zionists are not complete Jews until they reside in Israel. We must not leave aliyah to chance; rather we need an Israel-centered curriculum based on our heritage, culture, and language. Conservative congregations throughout America should develop youth, adult, and family Jewish Zionist education that heightens awareness of Israel and directly presents the option of aliyah. Specifically, the movement should issue (or reedit) textbooks on Israel and Zionist history for every age group, and usable in both formal and informal settings. Mercaz must be the guiding force in formulating this overall Zionist program.

Many Conservative *olim* participated in various programs sponsored by USY and Ramah. We should expand all these programs and create new ones, such as Ramah's High School Semester Program, which has attracted hundreds of young people and is growing. USY also should foster involvement in *ḥalutzim* and expand the options of such long-term programs in Israel as Nativ. There should be systematic and creative follow-up efforts for all who have returned from Israel programs.

We should place aliyah within the congregational calendar year. We might declare the Shabbat of *Parashat Lekh-lekha* as "Shabbat Aliyah." Rabbis throughout the country would focus on aliyah in their sermons and in Shabbat educational and social activities. Similarly, a Shabbat near Yom ha-Atzma'ut might involve a farewell ceremony for congregation members planning to make aliyah and for youth planning to go on summer programs in Israel. The movement must establish an ongoing dialogue with *olim*. For example, scholars-in-residence might be movement members who made aliyah and who would come on lecture tours and speak at the movement's national and local conventions.

Likewise, movement publications should be "fed" descriptions of absorption options (e.g., types of settlement and professional opportunities), along with accounts of exemplary absorption of *olim*.

Finally, the movement should establish a special fund to aid immigrants (especially singles) purchase apartments in Israel through supplementary mortgages. Loans should be available to single *olim*, who constitute forty-two percent of the aliyah from the West. Thus, the movement would be concretely involved in the upbuilding of Israeli society. Only through large-scale aliyah of its members will our movement influence the future course of Israeli society.

SUMMARY DIRECTIONS FOR THE FUTURE

Now that the Conservative Movement is an integral part of the World Zionist Organization, it must encourage aliyah as the ultimate fulfillment of Zionism, and as a viable option for each person. Mercaz, the movement's Zionist arm, must be the guiding force. I propose the following:

1. A curriculum on Israel based on our heritage, culture, and language, including specially designed Israel-centered textbooks and the other educational materials.
2. Strengthening Israel affairs committees.
3. Larger aliyah-support systems.
4. Summer and sabbatical family visits to Israel, family encampments there, and college-year and summer high school programs (including expanding the already-successful USY, Ramah, and Nativ programs).
5. Zionism and aliyah programs as part of congregational calendars (e.g., around Shabbat Lekh-Lekha and Yom ha-Atzma'ut).
6. Loan funds and second mortgages for Conservative olim.
7. A Conservative Movement Zionist periodical.

NOTES

1. Eliezer Schweid, *The Land of Israel: National Home or Land of Destiny* (New York: Herzl Press, 1985).
2. Alexander Barzel, *Lihyot Yehudi* [To be a Jew] (Kibbutz ha-Me'uḥad, 1985).
3. Ephraim E. Urbach, "Zionism: The Moral Obligation," in Moshe Davis (ed.), *Zionism in Transition* (New York: Herzl Press, 1980).
4. Arthur Hertzberg, *Being Jewish in America* (Jerusalem: Ha-Sifriyah ha-Tzionit, 1981).
5. Simon Halkin, *Unconditional Zionism* (Jerusalem: Ha-Sifriyah ha-Tzionit, 1985).
6. Natan Rotenstreich, *Examining Zionism Today* (Jerusalem: Ha-Sifriyah ha-Tzionit, 1977).
7. Arnold Eisen, paper published in *Towards a Zionist Renaissance* (Jerusalem: World Zionist Organization, 1987), p. 87.

SEMINAR 5

The Centrality of the State of Israel in Jewish Life

How should the State of Israel affect and penetrate the consciousness, liturgy, culture, and practice of Conservative Judaism in the Diaspora? Many leading Conservative Jews certainly have been passionate in their financial and political support of Israel. However, some have argued that, unfortunately, the state, its culture, and its society have exerted little genuine influence on other aspects of their Jewish lives. Is that characterization a fair one? Insofar as it is, what ought to be done to enrich and deepen the response of Conservative Jews to the existence and reality of the Jewish state in all its ramifications?

The Ambiguity of Our Ties to Israel

NEIL GILLMAN

I believe that a key issue in considering the State of Israel in Jewish life is not its centrality but its inherent *ambiguity*.

This derives largely from a prior ambiguity surrounding the place of the Land of Israel in Judaism. Like other religions, Judaism articulated a hierarchy of sacred spaces, all structured around the spot where God manifests Himself on earth. In its classical form, reading from the periphery to the center, the hierarchy was: the world, the land of Israel, the city of Jerusalem, the Temple, the Holy of Holies, the Ark, and, ultimately, the point between the two cherubim on the Ark's cover: "There I will meet with you and I will impart to you—from above the two cherubim that are on top of the Ark of the Pact—all that I will command you concerning the Israelite people" (Exodus 25:22; cf. Numbers 7:89). Appropriately, the later tradition (with the help of II Chronicles 3:1) identified the site of the Temple with Mount Moriah (or Adonai-yireh—literally, "the Lord will see"), the place where God appeared to Abraham as he prepared to sacrifice Isaac to the Lord (Genesis 22:14).

According to anthropologists of religion (e.g., Clifford Geertz and Mircea Eliade), this structuring of space is but one dimension of the broader task of religion, which is to cosmicize all of our experience, i.e., to bring order (or "cosmos") out of what would otherwise be anarchy (or "chaos," a state of undifferentiation).[1] Judaism recapitulates the more elaborate structuring of the world in the Creation of Genesis 1, and, of course, the structuring of time through biblical history and the liturgical year.

The structuring of space brings a sense of rootedness to the human community. While a warehouse may be perfectly adequate for storing cartons, human beings need homes, with rooms, walls separating one from the other, and specific functions assigned to each. A home conveys a sense of place, of belonging, and, therefore, of security—the safe "inside" as opposed to the perilous "outside." The mezuzah (or, in the Exodus narrative, the blood sprinkled on the doorposts and lintels of the house in 12:7) is the boundary between the two. Within this conceptualization, exile—i.e., displacement or banishment—becomes the paradigmatic punishment. Adam and Eve, and later Cain, were exiled for their sins (in Genesis 3–4); Cain properly understands that exile means increased vulnerability (4:14). The sense of his banishment from human society anticipates the portrayal of exile in the Deuteronomic *tokhaḥah* (curse) (28:36 ff.), which assumes that in exile "you shall serve other gods, of wood and stone." Exile is not only the symbol of utter futility; it also marks the severing of any link with God.

But the classic Jewish myth teaches that this entire structure was *overturned by God* as a punishment for our ancestors' sins. Twice, our sacred space was destroyed and our people banished from the center to the periphery. But this very same God, through His prophet Jeremiah (in his letter to the first community of exiles [chap. 29]), counsels that exile does not have to be the epitome of futility, the Deuteronomic vision notwithstanding: "Build houses . . . , plant gardens . . . , take wives . . . , beget sons and daughters . . . , multiply . . . , seek the welfare of the city . . . , prosper" (Jeremiah 29:5–7). These verses seem an explicit *reversal* of the *tokhaḥah*. The people, rather than worshipping gods of wood and stone in exile, are told: "When you call Me, and come and pray to Me, I will give heed to you. You will search for Me and find Me, if only you seek me wholeheartedly. I will be at hand for you . . . and I will restore your fortunes. And I will gather you from the nations . . . and I will bring you back to the place from which I have exiled you" (Jeremiah 29:13–14). The language has an emphatic, almost pleading, quality. The exiles may not have a Temple, they may not be permitted to perform the sacrificial cult, but they are hardly cut off from God.

Of course, God did bring them back to their land. As we know, however, most chose not to return, neither in Cyrus' time nor in Ezra and Nehemiah's, neither during the era of the Second Temple nor during the rest of Jewish history to our own day. Exile is a permanent fact of Jewish history—often *by choice*. Jeremiah's portrait of the exilic experience generally has proven to be singularly accurate. Other prophets established the religious framework of exile: Hosea's "For I desire goodness, not sacrifice (6:6); Amos' "I loath, I spurn your festivals. . . . But let justice well up like water" (5:21–41); and Isaiah's "What need have I of all your sacrifices? . . . That you come to appear before Me—who asked that of you? . . . Cease to do evil; learn to do good. Devote yourselves to justice; aid the wronged. Uphold the rights of the orphan; defend the cause of the widow" (1:11–12; 16–17).

After the destruction of the Second Temple in 70 C.E., this prophetic experience justified a complete transformation of Judaism's basic institutions. This transformation was sanctioned by God Himself, for the rabbis assumed that all of their halakhic decisions enjoyed God's explicit approval. The synagogue, the liturgy, the rabbinate, and particularly the halakhah, which transformed into an opportunity for worship every moment of lifetime for the Jew wherever he or she lived, became the central institutions of Jewish life. Every spot on earth was potentially the place of meeting between God and the Jews; every Jew was potentially the High Priest.

Above all, time—the day, the week, the month, the year, the life cycle—became the basis of cosmos, and thus, of sanctity. Space acquired a derivative sanctity; the Jew—not God—sanctified space in the form of a synagogue, a burial ground, even, to an extent, a home. None of these spaces enjoyed intrinsic sanctity. Any room could become a synagogue, any synagogue could be sold and a new one built, as Jews moved from one town to another.

What made this transformation possible was the notion of a monotheistic God. If God is truly sovereign of all of creation, then, as Jeremiah teaches, His power can be manifest even among the exiles. More important, He can be worshipped from any place on earth, not through sacrifices, but through prayer and halakhah.

The spaces that retained intrinsic sanctity—the land of Israel, Jerusalem, the site of the Temple—remained foci of yearning and devotion. But the rabbis assumed that only in the messianic future would Jews return there, a vision that was part of the broader restorative nature of the Jewish eschatological myth. In the interim, in history, Jewish religious existence reflected the tragic tension between the ideal and the real. On the one hand, there was the rich and variegated experience of the Jewish liturgical year; on the other, a sense of incompleteness, of an unredeemed world, of glasses broken at weddings, corners of rooms left unpainted, and morsels of food not eaten. In effect, Jews were told: Pray for the return to Zion, knowing that neither you nor your children ever will see it with your own eyes. In the meantime, "Acknowledge Him in all your ways." Aliyah may or may not be a mitzvah in theory, but it is clearly not accepted as one by many Diaspora Jews who claim to observe all of the mitzvot.

But Judaism is much more than a religion; it is a civilization centered about a people. It was the demands of peoplehood that impelled the emergence of modern political Zionism, and eventually, the establishment of the State of Israel. However ambivalent our purely *religious* impulses toward the land and the state, we must also contend with our *national* loyalties as Jews. We cannot help but identify strongly with those Jews who are citizens of the state, whose fate is intertwined with its. However *nationalist* the Zionist impulse may have been originally, paradoxically, for "religious" Jews, these national loyalties now are as intrinsic to Jewish *religious* life as the observing of the Sabbath, the festivals, and daily prayer. Can we identify with the fate of Israeli Jews without identifying with the fate of the State of Israel? Perhaps this identification too is a mitzvah. But how do we fulfill this mitzvah without making aliyah, which most of us simply are not going to do?

To complicate the issue more, we must ask: How do we express religious commitments to a community that often has contributed to the contemporary trivialization of the Jewish religion? For while the state has contributed much to enrich Jewish identity, it is of human authority and power, but mouthpieces of God. The kingdom is the antagonist, and we are required to identify with its Judge and Executioner. The view of the Second Temple period that has been shaped by tradition focuses not on the state of Judea (or the Roman province) but on the chain of Torah transmitters and the heroism of its defenders against the tide of Hellenism. For Judaism of post–Second Temple times the Torah was central. The kingdom (and the Land of Israel) were conceived of predominantly as instruments for the eventual fulfillment of the Torah in the messianic age.

In modern times the long humiliation of the Jews, capped by the Holocaust, exhausted the persuasiveness of the religious interpretation of exile as punishment (as, e.g., in the Musaf holy day liturgy). Some Jews took action and mobilized enough political, military, and economic force to establish the State of Israel—first of all as a haven for the body of the Jewish people, to save it from destruction, second as a haven for Jewish culture, to save it from dissipation. The success of the endeavor in political, military, and economic terms was striking; it served as compensation for the long humiliation and disgrace that preceded it. Jews were glad to take pride in the state and its achievements, to identify with it and bask in its glory. The horrible victimization of Jews that preceded the state lent a legitimation to its existence that was above criticism. The right of Jews to national peculiar existence had been denied; no challenges to that right could, in the light of the Holocaust, be justified in the eyes of Jews and many Gentiles.

Whatever blanket credit was given to the state in its earliest years has been eroded by the moral complications of power and of political and economic exigencies. Dispassionate inquiry into beginnings has revealed that Jewish activity in the prestate period was not free from moral ambiguity. Reflections have been made on the morality of the Zionist endeavor, echoing the Arab accusation that it was never anything but a land-robbing scheme. The denigration and delegitimization of Zionism is strengthened by present acts and omissions of the government of Israel that at least border on land-robbing and raise the specter of mass expulsion. In view of such doubts, the representative role of the state has become an embarassment to some Jews in Israel and outside it. To those for almost universally acknowledged to have cheapened the image of the Jewish religion, a classic instance of *ḥillul hashem* (desecration of God's name).

We American Jews live as complete and fulfilled a Jewish religious life as we wish, from the UJA-Federation "civil religionists" on the religious Left to the Satmar Hasidim on the Right. Nothing in the American environment *intrinsically* militates against where we locate ourselves on this continuum.

Of course, environment matters. Certain factors in the American environment will dilute a richer, more intensive Jewish religious life. But the same can be said for the Israeli Jews. While we contend with the perils of a much more open society, Israeli Jews face the temptation of allowing the Israeli mythic structure to substitute for the Jewish one, to claim that Judaism is superfluous in the Israeli setting. Each of us accepts our respective negative environmental influences as a trade-off for other positive values. For us, these include the excitement and enrichment of living within multiple civilizations; for Israelis, the intensification of the Jewish experience that becomes possible when Jewishness pervades the entire culture.

One expression of our Jewish religious commitment is identification with Israeli Jews and, derivatively, with the State of Israel. "Derivatively" indicates a readiness to be more critical toward the latter than to the former. For all Israeli Jews, as for all Jews everywhere, our love is unequivocal, regardless of how unhappy we may be with much of what the state stands for.

This unhappiness, however, must not detract from the way the state's establishment has led to the immeasurable enrichment of our Diaspora Jewish lives. Ultimately, Israel has accomplished two major goals: (1) providing a sanctuary for oppressed Jews from throughout the world, and (2) stimulating an unprecedented outpouring of Jewish cultural—though, sadly, not religious—creativity. Ahad Ha-Am was right: under conditions of self-determination, with Hebrew as the national language, and with the proper Jewish demographic density, Jewish culture has flourished as never before. There is nothing ambiguous about either of these accomplishments.

PROGRAMMATIC IMPLICATIONS

1. The terms "Zionist" and "Zionism" have lost their significance for those of us who choose to remain in the Diaspora; for Israelis, they have become an opprobrium. If we wish to use these terms, we must infuse them with more than minimalist content, more than signifying identification with the legitimacy of a state where Jews enjoy the fruits of self-determination.

2. We must address the issue of aliyah. Many Israeli officials who speak to American Jewish audiences imply that American Jewry is doomed, that Israel is the sole guarantor of Jewish survival. This rhetoric, which suggests a reality that simply is not so, demeans us all. Aliyah should be presented as *one* option for American Jews, but not as the only option. If we really accept that Jewish life today has two centers, each with its own strengths *and* shortcomings, we will have to reconceptualize why and how we teach aliyah.

3. We do not know how to celebrate *Yom ha-Atzma'ut*. We have no ritual, and our liturgies for the day are poor. Liturgies and rituals take time to evolve, but we should apply our creative resources in a systematic way to celebrate the day in an appropriately religious manner.

4. Most Jewish lay people have only the dimmest awareness of these last forty years' impact of Israel on Jewish scholarship and creativity. While we see Israeli scholars around our universities, the community at large knows little of their existence. We should organize conferences celebrating forty (or forty-five) years of Israeli Jewish scholarship, with sessions on Kaufmann, Scholem, as well as Epstein, Albeck, Urbach, and the other talmudists and historians such as Alon, Dinur, and their younger disciples. We should ask: How has the *fact* of the state affected Israeli scholarship? (To what extent has it led to tendentious interpretations of Jewish history?) We also should explore Israeli contributions to Hebrew letters, with sessions on Agnon, Oz, Appelfeld, Amichai, and others. In relation to this, we need more and better English translations of Israeli writers and scholars.

5. We must work hard to encourage the emergence of a more open, humanistic, and pluralistic understanding of Judaism for

Israeli Jews, and for the ultimate glorification of God, Torah, and Israel in the world.

SUMMARY

From a Jewish religious perspective, no matter how central the notion of an intrinsically sacred space may have been originally, Judaism's historical evolution rendered it superfluous. This evolution was explicitly sanctioned by God. Yet Judaism is more than a religion; its peoplehood dimension compels our loyalty to the Jews who inhabit that land, and, derivatively, to the state, the instrument of that community's self-determination. To complicate the issue further, for religious Jews, identification with the inhabitants of the state has a strong religious valence, but the image of Judaism emanating from the state has been largely negative. Thus multiple ambiguities lie at the heart of "the centrality of the State of Israel in Jewish life." For the foreseeable future, then, we must realize that there are two fully legitimate ways of being Jewish in history, each with its own source of enrichment and its inherent dangers. Each is immune from allegations of inauthenticity, and each needs the other's support.

NOTE

1. One example is the highly structured Israelite camp in the otherwise barren wilderness, described in Numbers 2–3.

The Task of Masorti Judaism

MOSHE GREENBERG

As the sole political entity created by the combined and concentrated efforts of the Jewish people, the State of Israel is willy-nilly the most salient achievement of the Jewish people in our time. Jews and gentiles alike regard the state as representing the Jewish people as a whole. The conduct of the state reflects on Jews everywhere, as the treatment of Jews everywhere is of concern to the state. In this way, for the individual Jew, the state is a constant presence, more or less salient in proportion to one's Jewishness. In its distress, the state may take a central position in the consciousness of all Jews in its symbolic status as their representative. In addition, for its citizens, the state is the organism by which their lives are ordered and governed; not a symbol but an authority and a power for bettering their daily lives or for worsening them. For its citizens the state is a complex entity: it is the condition of their mundane well-being (which it is not for other Jews), and more abstractly it serves as the collective portrait of its Jewish inhabitants, who control it and set its policy and conduct, and who are seen (and see themselves) as the vital kernel of the Jewish people as a whole.

Jews in Israel and outside it share, then, the estimate of the state as somehow expressing the essence of the Jewish people. Jewish identity is inextricably bound up with the state. This is a new thing in the history of Jews and Judaism. The Bible pits allegiance to God and His commands against the waywardness of people and kingdom: its heroes are not mouthpieces of the kingdom, organs whom Jewish identity and Judaism are inseparable, the perceived immorality of the state's conduct introduces a painful wedge between the state and their self-image as Judaistic Jews (Jews vitally committed to the perpetuation of Judaism). Something of the biblical opposition to the ancient Israelite kingdoms comes to mind. Indeed one may play with the notion that for the health of Judaism the state is dangerous. The program of the anti-Zionist Neturei Karta sect becomes intelligible.

Another source of conflict between Jewish identity and the state is the state-authorized monopoly over institutions of religion enjoyed by Orthodoxy. Such a monopoly would be irritating even if it were exercised liberally; it is insufferable in the increasingly sectarian spirit of its present exercise. Intolerant rigorism, constantly seeking new conflicts with those oustide the sect, is rapidly rousing general revulsion against all that savors of Judaism in the populace at large. For all but rigoristic Orthodox Jews the collusion of the state in their monopoly is alienating.

In these circumstances it is important to clarify what a Judaistic Jewishness considers the centrality of the state to mean. I do not think there is a difference between citizen and outlander in this matter.

The function of the Jewish state in Judaism is to promote the realization of Torah in life and society; if it fails to do that, or acts against that purpose, it forfeits its right to exist. The state is an instrument to an end.

The scope of Torah is total. Its ideal is to permeate life and society and shape all to the service and the greater glorification of God (*kiddush hashem*).

To Orthodoxy, realization of the Torah means effectuating halakhah as it appears in the codes and responsa, and as currently interpreted by authorized *musmachim*. But Orthodoxy's program is impracticable. First, because of the obsolescence of halakhah—whose evolution lags behind civilization—and of halakhists—whose training is narrowly clerical and gives them no grasp of the complexity of modernity (e.g., the interaction of technological advance and ethics; the effect of historical knowledge on ancient authority). Second, because halakhah claims the right of coercion to its totalitarian system, a claim which, given halakhic obsolescence, is firmly resisted by the modern-minded, who constitute the bulk of Jewry. Halakhah and halkhists may theoretically catch up with modernity (if, that is, they are forced to by, or wish to address, a modern-minded constituency that has as its ideal the permeation of life—not merely the cult—by halakhah), but in the meanwhile the Jewishness of the Jewish state cannot be expressed by Orthodoxy's cultic monopoly.

For the Judaistic Jew (in and out of the state) the State of Israel is the optimum location for probing the validity of Judaism (understood as the fullness of Jewish expression through the ages, not merely halakhah) as a comprehensive Torah of life (*torat ḥayyim*). Outside the state the springs of valuation in given national contexts are secular, Christian, Muslim, Marxist, Hindu, etc., and combinations thereof. Diaspora Jewish communities are primarily identified as cultic associations whose distinctive values pertain to the private realm; the public realm amidst which they live is governed by the above-mentioned springs of value. The Jewish state offers the only arena in which Jewish-Torah values can play on public issues (sharing the field, to be sure, with competing claimants, as elsewhere).

How does the state offer such an arena? By providing an environment in which the temporal rhythm is Jewish, Jewish self-knowledge is avidly pursued, and education (through schools, communications media, and adult voluntary associations) routinely takes great account of Jewish literature and history.

- The state calendar is Jewish: the week ends with the Sabbath day of rest; national and commercial holidays are Jewish (you may go to the beach, but it is Rosh Hashanah, not Labor Day). Life rhythms are therefore perforce Jewish, and the media constantly offer programs and notices of the Jewish moments of the year.
- Cultivation of Jewish self-knowledge is a universal value in the state: Hebrew, as the key to continuity with the Jewish heritage and the historic common bond of all Jewish communities, is the national language. Research into Jewish ethnography, history, literature, archaeology, sociology, economics, art, and all other forms of Jewish self-expression is publicly valued

and supported (e.g., through institutions of higher learning and research, archives, and museums).
- Educational institutions include as a matter of course a curriculum in Jewish classics: the Bible, Talmud and Midrash, medieval Jewish thought. The public school systems include these subjects in their curriculums; the media regularly offer bits of these classics.

Now it is the general expectation that this exposure of the public, from childhood on, to Jewish things will create a setting in which a Jewish culture will emerge, participating to be sure in general world civilization, but displaying a distinctively Jewish character. General world civilization is a lowest common denominator of technology and culture that confers no specific identity, engages no sentiments of loyalty and commitment, creates no communities sharing a way of life and whose members are mutually supporting. General world civilization offers no hallowed symbols of the transcendent, no life-regimen and rituals by which the individual and the community may express the universal human intuition that there is a realm beyond the sensible and countable, a realm from which all value springs, and contact with which is the ultimately worthwhile.

Nor does the secular world-view of modernity, with its boundless choices and its self-centered individualism, offer real guidance concerning value commitments:

- whether to be faithful to the marriage bond;
- whether to be honest in business;
- whether to fulfill obligations conscientiously;
- whether to be considerate of the unfortunate.

It is the expectation of the Jewish public that exposure to Jewish sources will generate good conduct and loyalty to the community. And it is the consequence of the peculiarly congenial setting of Israel for acquiring knowledge of Jewish sources and exposure to their content throughout life that Jews everywhere expect good conduct and communal loyalty to be a prominent feature of Israel society. When these effects are not visible many Israelis feel guilty and, with Diaspora Jewry, feel they are dishonoring Judaism (*ḥillul hashem*).

Of itself exposure to Jewish sources is no guarantee of right(eous) conduct. The sources contain a vast mixture of perennial values and contingent embodiments of them—including deficient embodiments that even for their own times were recognized as such (e.g., the amazement expressed in the Mekhilta at the rabbinic exegesis of Exodus 21:14 that exempted the murderer of a gentile from prosecution). The inability of Orthodoxy to acknowledge the conditional character of many aspects of Jewish tradition (allowing, e.g., the current flourishing of religious xenophobia); its refusal to seek within the tradition principles by which to establish a hierarchy of values—priorities necessary when life-situations—communal life-and-death situations as well as individual ones—require preferring one value over another (the integrity of Eretz Yisrael vs. the integrity of Am Yisrael); Orthodoxy's tendency to stress ritual over moral scrupulousness—all these render it incapable of showing the way the state can exploit its unique resources for the promotion of Judaism as a guide to life. In this crisis of Judaism—public need and expectation stultified by the paralysis of its official custodians—Masorti opportunity, indeed responsibility and obligation, is patent.

Nothing less is at stake than the Jewish character of the state, given the determined opposition of the majority of its citizens to the coercive Orthodox conception and the absence of a coherent alternative conception. Consequently the significance (if not centrality) of Israel for Diaspora Jewry is also at stake: for neither the dead hand of Orthodoxy nor the vague, shallow Jewish-style secularism proffered by the present-day Israeli culture can speak to Judaistic Diaspora Jews whose attachment to Torah and Judaism seeks a modern expression and environment. The Masorti Movement's proper task is to promote energetically the fulfillment of the general Jewish expectation that the State of Israel will be the seedbed of a full Jewish life that

- for the individual and the private realm prescribes a regimen that relates the individual to the transcendent (God and Torah) through study, prayer, and the practice of *mitzvot ben adam*

la-makom; relates the individual to family in bonds of loyalty and mutual respect; relates the individual to society as a participant in its upbuilding and defense, through whose acts God and Torah are honored.
- for the society promotes a self-conception of the Jewish people and the state as called to the service of a universal purpose: to be an instrument of upbuilding humanity, through examples of justice, compassion, and harmony, to regard ourselves as trustees of a sacred heritage, hence to take account, in all communal/national decisions, of how our conduct reflects on our heritage (bringing contumely on ourselves is a betrayal of trust—*ḥillul hashem*).

The Masorti movement will promote these ends if and as it generates scholars and rabbis who can interpret and sift the heritage in accord with the times and whose conduct exemplifies the fullness of individual Jewish life above-sketched; and as its spiritual leaders inspire communities to form around synagogue-centers that will breed a citizenry exemplifying in their conduct individual Jewish virtues and carrying into public and civic life the ideal of the state as an instrument to fulfill a universal purpose.

As the embodiment of striving to fulfill Jewish ideals, the Masorti Movement will offer a link with all Jews whose Jewish identity includes both particular and universal values. The ideal basis and expression of that link will be

- a shared individual way of life (regimen of *mitzvot ben adam la-makom*);
- bilingualism: as every Israeli finds it necessary to have a diasporal language (most often English), so every diasporal Jew who seeks to link himself with the only community in which Judaism engages the fullness of life situations must acquire the Hebrew language;
- shared commitment that individually and communally Jews will reflect honor on Judaism (*kiddush hashem*);
- shared hope that Israel and the Diaspora will thrive in peace among the gentiles.

The last two items ought to be incorporated in the liturgy, as instituted hope and commitments of all Jewish communities.

Ought there to be a shared hope for the ingathering of all Diasporas to the State of Israel? To the extent that Diaspora Jewry is permeated with the Jewish heritage, in which this hope is everpresent; to the extent that the Israeli community is attractive as a laboratory for the realization of Judaism, one can look for a constant movement of idealistic individuals to Israel seeking to fulfill their Jewishness. To cut out prayers for the ingathering would mean a major break in the continuity of Jewish self-definition. Since Israeli Jewry has no reason to favor such a move, it will come, if it does, from Diaspora communities. But not until these have undergone such an attenuation of Jewish identity as will in any case relegate the State of Israel to a remote corner of life, perhaps like Mecca an object of pilgrimage once in a lifetime.

SUMMARY

The centrality of the State of Israel for the Jewish people (if not for every Jew) is a fact of modern Jewish existence. But the moral quandaries of the state and its grant of a monopoly on official religion to rigorous Orthodoxy distress Jews for whom humane Judaism and modernity are a vital concern (henceforth called Judaistic Jews). In this situation what may such Jews envisage as the basis of their attachment to the state?

The State of Israel offers a unique setting to probe the validity of Judaism as a guide to life, since its basic cultural resources, publicly promoted through educational institutions and the media, are Hebraic and Judaistic. No other culture (e.g., general secular civilization) can confer a specific identity on the Israeli Jew, so he is thrown perforce on the heritage of Judaism. Since the mediation of that heritage by Orthodoxy is unacceptable to the majority of Jews in and out of Israel, both the Jewish character of the state and its significance for the spiritual life of diaspora Jewry are at issue.

The Masorti movement in Israel promises to answer the expectation of Jews everywhere that the Jewish state will produce a voice speaking for its humane Jewish character. It must promote the fulfillment of the general Jewish expectation that the state will be the seedbed of a full Jewish life expressed

- in the individual sphere by a regimen that relates the individual to the transcendent (*mitzvot ben adam la-makom*), and to family and society in an honorable, constructive manner;
- in the communal/national sphere through the self-conception of the Jewish people as called to the service of a universal purpose, to be an exemplary people, the trustees of a sacred heritage.

Such a movement may hope to link Judaistic Jews of the Diaspora to Israel. For such a link to be forged, both communities must possess these features:

- a shared life-regimen of mitzvot;
- a commitment to *kiddush hashem* (in the everyday sense);
- bilingualism (Hebrew plus);
- shared hope for the peaceful thriving of Israel and the Diaspora.

The last two items ought to be embodied in the liturgy.

The Actualization of the Traditional View of Israel's Centrality

REUVEN HAMMER

My approach to the topic "The Centrality of the State of Israel in Jewish Life" is philosophic-theological, i.e., a focus on the place of a Jewish homeland in Judaism. The heading of this section posits Israel as "central," as occupying a place of great prominence, which rules out other places of Jewish life having equal prominence.

The Masorti Movement, as a Zionist movement, also views the return of the Jewish people to its land as the central event of modern Jewish history. Thus, Israel might be viewed as central both in terms of recent Jewish history and in terms of Jewish life today.

The centrality of the State of Israel frequently is argued on the basis of the Jewish people's survival. Herzl and others contended that the tenacity and virulence of anti-Semitism made the Jews' future outside of Palestine questionable; since the *Shoah* (Holocaust), it is not easy to dismiss this argument. The leaders of historical and Conservative Judaism, such as Zechariah Frankel and Solomon Schechter, argued that there were many places in which Jews could not live freely, and that Jews from such lands should have their own land in Israel. However, they believed that those who could live freely in their motherland, such as Germany (Frankel) or America (Schechter), should do so. Basically this has been the approach of American Zionists and of the Conservative Movement (the latter as reflected in its liturgy).

It also has been argued that Israel provides a better place for Jews to flourish spiritually and culturally than the Diaspora, for here Judaism is not threatened by assimilation or intermarriage. In America, where the Jew may feel physically safe, he may not be spiritually secure; he may be lost in the country's pluralist, largely secular democracy, as Hillel Halkin has noted.[1] Schechter, following Ahad Ha-Am, acknowledges that the spiritual danger in America is indeed great, but that it can be counteracted by creating a spiritual/cultural center in Palestine which can serve as the chief support of Jewish life in the Diaspora. This spiritual center would obviate the need for Jews in free countries to move to Palestine. Israel Friedlander also looked forward to the spiritual benefits which a renewed Jewish state could bring. He felt that while the Diaspora might secure emancipation and physical survival for Jews, "we scarcely hope for a creative Judaism" there—damning words indeed.[2]

Even Abraham Joshua Heschel's wonderful book *Israel,* in which he came to terms with the need for holiness in space (place)[3] as well as in time, expounded the meaning of the state largely in terms of how it inspires Jews who live elsewhere: "There is a cure of the souls in the concern on the part of the Jews everywhere for the people who live in the State of Israel. . . . Such care may serve as an example to all mankind."[4] It is only on the penultimate page of the book that he says, "Not living in the land, nonparticipation in the drama, is a source of embarrassment." Obviously it is an "embarrassment" which many people can endure quite nicely.

The problem with such approaches is that, traditionally, Judaism views the existence of the center in the land of Israel neither in terms of its benefits for other Jewries nor as a physical haven for Jews in danger, but in terms of its intrinsic value. The Torah envisions the creation of the Kingdom of God in the land not so that those who live elsewhere (Galut) can continue to be Jews, but because the existence of the Jewish people there is necessary for the fulfillment of the divine plan. Here is a utopian, not a practical, perspective on the centrality of Israel in Jewish life: a Jewish state becomes an end, not a means.

The Torah relates God's search for a people who will be His people, who will actualize His will on earth. To this people, He promises a land in which they will be able to fulfill this task. The greatest punishment envisioned for this people is to be driven from that Land (Deuteronomy 28:63 ff.). As later rabbinic tradition put it succinctly: "Dwelling in the Land of Israel is equivalent to observing all of the Torah's commandments" (Sifre Deuteronomy, piska 80).

The biblical vision is fulfilled through a two-stage development— the first being the covenant with the Patriarchs, in which God promises each in turn that he will become the father of a populous people, will be granted the land, and will become a blessing to all mankind (Genesis 12:2–3). As M. Weinfeld has pointed out, this is a one-sided covenant; it is granted as a gift to Abraham in return for his loyalty and steadfastness to God (of which the Akedah [binding of Isaac—see Genesis 22] is the prime example), but nothing is required of Abraham or his descendants. The assumption, however, is that the latter will continue in Abraham's way, will be loyal to God, and will live just and righteous lives.

After the Exodus, a second covenant is promulgated which develops, but is radically different from, the first. The people have the option of accepting God's kingship, in return for which God will be their God and they will be His special people, and will be permitted to live in the land (Exodus 19:4–6). The relationship is contingent upon their following God's ways, which are translated into specific commandments. The granting of the land is not simply the gift of a place to live, which, as Amos points out (9:7), God has done for many nations, but the opportunity to actualize the meaning of being His people through the creation of a Godly society in this chosen place. The ultimate reward is to lengthen one's days upon the land which the Lord gives one (Exodus 20:12). The confession of the first fruits (Deuteronomy 21) expressed the belief that the fulfillment of the covenant occurs when one has the fruits of the land in his hand.

Again and again, the Bible makes a connection between leaving Egypt and coming to the land, with the purpose of making God our King. The idea is repeated in Nehemiah 9:6–11, which observant Jews recite every day before Shirat ha-Yam (the Song of the Sea— see Exodus 15) or in the verses recited before Ashrei: "The Lord chose Zion. He desired it for His habitation. The Lord chose

Jacob, Israel as His special treasure. The Lord will not cast aside His people. He will not desert his portion." Note the consistent parallelism between the land and the people Israel. As Heschel wrote in *Israel*, "To abandon the land would be to repudiate the Bible."[5]

Even when historical circumstances made it impossible for us to be centered in the Land following the Bar Kokhba revolt, we were able to forge instruments which permitted us to live elsewhere without loss of identity. But these instruments were not seen as permanent replacements for the land.[6]

To understand this, one needs to look more at the role of the land in the Jewish tradition. There is a long-standing halakhic dispute on whether leaving the Golah (Diaspora) and going on aliyah (immigrating to Israel) is a mitzvah (commandment). The Rambam (Maimonides) does not include it as a mitzvah, while the Ramban (Nachmanides) does. In his commentary to Numbers 23:53 the Ramban writes, "In my opinion this is a positive commandment . . . and this command is repeated in many places."[7] I feel that this may be a perfect case for applying the Franz Rosenzweig principle, i.e., that the command applies when one feels that he/she is commanded. Those who do not go should give his classic answer when asked whether they are fulfilling this commandment: not yet. While the mitzvah exists for each individual, not every individual is capable of fulfilling it. However, the Jewish people—the people of Israel—is commanded to establish its nation in Eretz Yisrael and nowhere else.[8] The Torah and the words of the prophets are meaningless unless this premise is granted.

Certain Christian theologians maintain that this idea is outdated and has been superseded. They posit that there is an Old and a New Testament, and that the New has freed mankind from the constraints of the Old, including its land-bound nature. Jews cannot agree, however. They can say: not now, not yet, not everybody. Not now—wait for the Messiah until all Jews are "ingathered" in the Land. Not yet—conditions must be ripe. Not everybody—Jews can exist as Jews in other places as well as in Israel. Otherwise, Judaism would stop at the border and any Jew who left, for any reason whatsoever, would cease to be a Jew—a kind of reverse Law of Return. Clearly that is absurd. The possibility of Jewish existence outside the land was demonstrated in the Book of Joshua, in a passage where the tribes outside the land feared that they would not be considered Israelites by those inside. They took the strange and desperate action of building a totally useless altar to serve as a symbol of their membership in the community of Israel (Joshua 22:9 ff.). During the Second Temple period, there were extensive Jewish communities in the Diaspora, a phenomenon that, notably, classical Jewish texts failed to condemn. Yet such communities, no matter how strong, could never fulfill the divine covenant which is the ultimate goal mandated by the Torah.

The individual Jew, then, may or may not be obligated to live in Zion. The people of Israel is commanded to establish itself there in order to actualize the Kingdom of God. The individual Jew is commanded to observe the mitzvot wherever he is. But there are limitations to what he can do outside the land, for the quality of sacredness is diminished in the Diaspora.[9] The most extreme expression of this is found in the Sifre to Deuteronomy: "Even though I am about to exile you from the land to a foreign land, you must continue to be marked there by the commandments, so that when you return they will not be new to you" (Pesikta 43). The authentic place for observance is in the land and there alone; everything else is imitation and preparation.

Traditional Judaism can envision Diaspora Jewish communities, but grants them a diminished status, certainly nothing comparable to living in the land. While Jews are commanded to pray for the peace of the land in which they live, to follow its law (except when it contradicts Judaism's basic beliefs), the reason given is only "so that people will not swallow each other alive."[10]

But all Jews pray for the land of Israel in the regular formula of prayer ordained by the sages. Examples are manifold: "Return to Your city, Jerusalem," "sound the great shofar for our freedom," breaking the glass at the end of a wedding,[11] the recitation of "next year in Jerusalem" at the end of Yom Kippur and of the Passover Seder, and the blessing of the new month, when we pray: "He who wrought miracles for our ancestors and redeemed them from slavery unto freedom, may He redeem us speedily and gather our exiles from the four corners of the world, for all Israel are brethren."

Try reciting the daily prayers with this in mind and see how many passages referring to the land leap to the fore. Yet the clarity of this commitment is lost in mistranslated or obfuscated passages, e.g., the Rosh Hodesh blessing in the Bokser Siddur:

> May He, who wrought wondrous deeds for our ancestors, and delivered them from slavery to freedom, bring a speedy redemption unto us from all the ills which oppress our lives. May He gather the homeless of our people and plant them again firmly in their own land. O may friendship link the people of Israel into an enduring fellowship.

The "translation" in *Sim Shalom* of the prayer in the daily Amidah, "Sound the great shofar proclaiming our freedom, raise the banner to gather our exiles and gather us together from the four corners of the world," reads: "gather the dispersed from the ends of the earth."

It is possible for Jews to exist elsewhere—provided they help assure the settlement of the land, and they do not lose a close connection with it. But they do not have full participation in the Torah's plan while living in exile.[12] As a holy people who can realize their holiness only in their only land, the Jews are commanded to populate the land. Their not doing so in the incident of the spies (Numbers 13–14) was accounted a great sin, which led to forty years' additional wandering in the desert.

The centrality of the State of Israel, then, lies primarily neither in providing a safe place where Jews can live (important as that is) nor in serving as the location where Judaism in all manifestations can best flourish. Rather, it consists in being the focus for the realization of the Torah's ultimate goal, as reiterated by the prophets and reaffirmed in rabbinic literature: God has found this people to be His people, and they will only fully fulfill His will in the land. While all observance of Judaism outside of the land is important and should be encouraged, such observance does not have the same status as the people's fulfillment of its central mission. Therefore, it clearly is incumbent upon us to encourage aliyah so that the individual can participate in this mitzvah of the people and the people can fulfill itself.

It seems to me crucial that this view be reflected in the literature of the Conservative Movement, be it in *Emet ve-Emunah,* periodicals we issue, or prayerbooks and Haggadot. Translations which gloss over the traditional viewpoint must be rectified. A liturgy for Yom ha-Atzma'ut (Israeli Independence Day) should be created which reflects these concepts so that they become integral to each Jew's religious consciousness.

Likewise, our school curricula should emphasize the centrality of Israel, e.g., in viewing the Exodus as having implications for today, not as mere Bible study. Similarly, the Torah should be studied not only in terms of a holiness code containing guidelines for moral or religious rituals and holy days, but as a vision of progressing toward a holy society with specific socioeconomic steps along the way (e.g., the Jubilee laws, richly detailed yet often observed in the breach). Jewish historical development might then be studied from the perspective of how this vision was developed or perverted. The lives of all nations, ancient and modern, can then be judged in terms of how they compare to the Bible's goal of a land-based utopia.

The adoption of the centrality of Israel in Conservative theology demands that the movement redefine and restructure itself. It calls for moving the physical center of the movement to Israel, for the construction of a world headquarters in Jerusalem (which the Reform Movement did years ago). What is involved is more a mental than a physical process, requiring that we stop perceiving Judaism and Jewish life through American eyes.

Through words and, above all, through action, Conservative Judaism must proclaim that the natural and complete fulfillment of covenantal Judaism is attainable only in Israel.

1. Every teenager should spend a summer in Israel under the supervision of Ramah or USY.
2. Every college-age student should spend a year in Israel in Midreshet Yerushalayim, Nativ, or some other appropriate program.
3. Every family should have a program of living and studying in

Israel for a minimum of a month or possibly for a summer or a year. A special new agency of the movement should coordinate arrangements, programs, and follow-up.
4. A fund to help those who wish to make aliyah should be established.

At the least, every Jew should spend some significant period of time in Israel. Only after doing so can he/she make an informal choice to decide whether to become an integral part of the Jewish State or to contribute to the biblical vision from outside its borders.

For those Jews who remain in the Golah (Diaspora), this reordering of the Jewish world-view will at the very least help them understand that Judaism speaks not only to individuals but to communities, so that *every* society must be judged by its adherence to God's demands. It also will unite Jews in common concern for an Israel now more sharply signified as the "Jewish center."

It will provide a method of judging which organizations and groups in Israel are worthy of support. By participating in such organizations and strengthening the Israel which is true to the biblical and rabbinic vision, the individual will be participating in the enterprise of the Jewish nation.

SUMMARY

The centrality and importance of Israel traditionally has been viewed in terms of the physical or spiritual survival of the Jewish people. For some, this meant the ingathering of all Jews and the concomitant abolishment of Jewry outside of Israel. American Zionist thinkers, however, maintained that if Israel flourished, this would strengthen American Jewish life. For both viewpoints, the emphasis was on what Israel could do for Diaspora Jewry.

The classical sources of Judaism, however, are concerned with Israel not in terms of what it can do for other Jewish communities, but because of the land's intrinsic value as the means of fulfilling the divine plan. The covenant of Israel with God demands the establishment of a nation-community in Eretz Yisrael which will actualize His will; that is the ultimate purpose of the Exodus.

A reading of the Bible from any view but this one is distorted.

Similarly, the Siddur expressed these ideas time and again, although American translations often seek to obscure its land-centered allusions.

This basic land-centered focus of the Bible and of Rabbinic Judaism impels us to give Israel a high position on the agenda of Conservative Jewry in America and elsewhere. This can be done via the following:

1. Accurate translations of the prayers.
2. Honest teaching of the Bible's focus on Eretz Yisrael.
3. A liturgy for Yom ha-Atzma'ut which reflects this focus.
4. Various movement publications stressing the creation and sustaining of Israel as the supreme task of the Jewish people, and the responsibility of each individual to contribute to Israel's well-being.
5. A focus on Israel in the curricula of our schools.
6. Centralization of the movement physically in Israel.
7. Bringing every Conservative teenager and college student to Israel.
8. Bringing families to Israel for appropriate programs.
9. Creating an aliyah fund.

For those who choose to remain outside the center, this program will at least provide a focus of activity and will support the view that Judaism is concerned not only with individuals, but with societies and their adherence to God's demands.

NOTES

1. See Hillel Halkin, *Letters to an American Jewish Friend* (Philadelphia: Jewish Publication Society, 1977).

2. Israel Friedlander, *Past and Present* (New York: Burning Bush Press, 1961), p. 320.

3. With regard to the holiness of place, the Torah and the rabbis were rather careful about ascribing holiness to places except where God was present. Thus Sinai is holy when God is there, either at the bush or at the revelation. The place of the sanctuary is holy, even the portable one, because God is there. Moriah or Zion becomes holy and, by extension, Jerusalem, when the Tabernacle, the portable Sinai, is established there permanently and God's Presence fills it (I Kings 8). In our day, we see how too much "place holiness" can lead to zealotry, but its excesses should not prove an idea's illegitimacy.

4. Abraham Joshua Heschel, *Israel* (New York: Farrar, Straus, Giroux, 1969), p. 211.

5. Ibid., p. 44.

6. Some Zionists have seen all of Jewish religious life as only *kelei golah,* i.e., artificial substitutes suitable only for Diaspora life and discardable upon the return to Zion. This is "the other side of the coin" and as much of an error as seeing them as instruments by which Judaism freed itself of the need for a land of its own, e.g., of seeing America as "our Jerusalem."

7. See *The Talmudic Encyclopedia* (Hebrew), vol. 2 (Jerusalem: Talmudic Encyclopedia Publishing, 1956), p. 223, for a full discussion of *yishuv ha-aretz,* the command to dwell in the land.

8. See Walter Brueggemann, *The Land* (Philadelphia: Fortress Press, 1977), esp. pp. 5–6, for a survey of the biblical position on settling the Land; also A. Roy Eckhardt, *For Righteousness' Sake* (Bloomington: Indiana University Press, 1987), and W. R. Davis, *The Gospel and the Land* (Los Angeles: University of California Press, 1974).

9. Babylonian Talmud, M. Kidushin, end of chap. 1.

10. In the USSR, I saw prayerbooks which contained prayers for Emperor Franz Joseph and witnessed Jews praying for the USSR itself, which shows the absurd lengths to which this can go.

11. Signifying some sorrow, even amid joy, for the Temple's destruction and the resulting exit from the land.

12. A complication to a God-oriented land during the biblical era was the people's desire for a king. This contradicted the belief in God as King, but this arrangement not only was accepted, but was turned into a basic pillar of Judaism (see I Samuel 8). Today, a similar problem arises, for a democratically established state in which non-Jews have equal rights is quite different from a state whose policies are shaped by divine commands. This has led a number of thinkers, including Yeshayah Leibowitz, to argue that the state has no religious value whatsoever. While Leibowitz is a feisty extremist, he provides a counterweight to the tendency toward deification of the state. For the state should not be worshipped any more than the Kotel (Western Wall) should be worshipped; it is of worth only as an instrument toward the Jewish values we cherish.

SEMINAR 6

Peace, Land, and Security in the State of Israel

Probably more than any other topic at this conference, American Jewish thinkers have devoted more intellectual, political, and emotional energy to this issue. The questions here are both familiar and numerous: What general approach should Israel adopt in its search for peace? What should be its ultimate goals, strategy, and tactics? How much weight should be given to sovereign control of land above and beyond its value in security terms? How perilous is the occupation to Israel's Judaic, humanitarian, and democratic character? What are the true intentions of the Palestinians and other Arabs, and how may they be influenced?

Whatever we may think about these ideas, all of which seriously divide Israeli policy-makers, what should Diaspora Conservative Jews say and do about them? Should we express our views on these matters of contention within Israel? If so how, where, and to whom? What are the dangers of "speaking out," and what are the dangers of not "speaking out"?

The Need for a New Zionism

PHILIP SPECTRE

One can identify five distinct proposed solutions to the Israel-Palestinian conflict. Each raises strong objections. By identifying these, one can clarify what the Masorti/Conservative Movement can contribute to the peace process.

AUTONOMY

In 1978, the Camp David Agreement included autonomy as an interim stage towards independence for the Palestinians. It calls for local civil authorities elected by the territories' Palestinian residents to administer the municipal and rural service departments, including a police force. Israel would continue to control security and water resources.

The Likud Party has since developed a somewhat different interpretation of autonomy, which it views not as an interim stage, but as an end in itself. Israel would allow the Palestinians certain rights while it annexes the territories. However, they would remain nonvoting and "citizenless" residents.

For right-wing parties such as Techiya or Kach,[1] any lessening of Israel's authority over the Arabs is reprehensible, if not treasonous. Similarly, any step toward the creation of a Palestinian state encourages terrorist elements and weakens Israel's future.

For left-wing parties, such as Ratz or Mapam, the Likud's view of annexation totally distorts the meaning of the word "autonomy." Although autonomy as an interim step might be helpful, they fear that if the Arabs continue to live in the occupied territories without complete rights, Israel's "Palestinian problem" will continue to fester.

ESTABLISHING A PALESTINIAN STATE

Israel would withdraw from all occupied territories, except for East Jerusalem and the Golan Heights, and allow the Palestinian leadership to form an independent state.

For parties on the right, this option constitutes capitulation. They predict that Israel will face doom when the new state, hostile to Israel and strengthened by other Arab countries and the superpowers, attacks Israel.

Religious right-wing parties cannot allow the Holy Land to fall under the sovereignty of non-Jews. This diminishing of "Greater Israel" is viewed by them as a sin.

Likud, believing that settlements in the territories strengthen Israel's security, also refuse to give them up. Many Israelis across the political spectrum fear that withdrawal will facilitate the creation of a base for terrorism and jeopardize the IDF's ability to repel a sneak attack.

Were an independent Palestinian state established, it would be extremely weak and dependent upon either superpower support or one of its Arab neighbors. In short, opponents of a Palestinian state claim that Israel, through its establishment, will only increase its vulnerability.[2]

A JORDANIAN/PALESTINIAN STATE

Recent proclamations by King Hussein have made this option quite unlikely. However, factions in Israel and elsewhere long have claimed that Jordan is Israel's most promising partner for the next phase of peace negotiations.

Under this plan Jordan, in coordination with the Palestinian leadership,[3] would repossess much of the territory lost to Israel after the wars of 1948 and 1967. It would establish either an expanded Jordan in cooperation with the Palestinian leadership in the West Bank or a confederation between Jordan and a new Palestinian entity.

In addition to the objections raised to *any* Palestinian entity, the problem of Jerusalem becomes acute. Under this proposed option, Jordan always has insisted on the return of Jerusalem as a first step toward any negotiated peace process.

Although this arrangement would be more stable than a state formed by Palestinians alone, many Israelis fear that no enduring political entity would be formed. Strife between two such weak partners would result in superpower intervention, so that Israel will only be exacerbating an already impossible situation on its borders.

INCORPORATION OF THE TERRITORIES WITHIN ISRAEL

Were Israel to annex the territories, as it has done with Jerusalem and the Golan Heights, it could take unilateral action towards solving its border problems without negotiating with the Palestinians.

Yet annexation of the territories also would bring an additional 1,150,000 Arabs under Israeli rule, or about forty percent of Israel's total population. This "demographic time bomb," the left-wing political parties feel, would soon produce an Arab majority in Israel.

Labor and the other left-wing parties also fear that unilateral annexation irreparably would alienate the Arab leadership. They believe that Egypt would annul its peace agreement and join the Arab League in viewing annexation as a *causus belli*. Thus, annexation would thwart Israeli peace initiatives, and Israel would end up even more isolated than it is today.

THE STATUS QUO

By making no political or military initiatives, Israel would maintain the status quo of occupying territories gained in the Six-Day War without negotiating with any of the parties. Arabs in the territories would not be given further rights, but no annexation would take place.

Yet as Palestinian Arab frustration grew, unrest would increase. Israel's reserve army increasingly would be taxed by uprisings, strikes, and terrorist activities, weakening its ability to protect the country against preemptive strikes.

As the occupation continues, the Arab states might form a united front against Israel. Hussein's recent yielding of sovereignty over the West Bank might be viewed as a step in that direction.

CONCLUSIONS

The above options have three major common elements: (1) religious/messianic imperatives; (2) moral concerns; and (3) security issues. Two of these should be eliminated from our discussion, so that our analysis may focus solely on the third.

The religious/messianic imperative is of little significance to the Conservative/Masorti Movement. Among our rabbis and laypeople, very few claim that religion should mandate territorial policy. No claim for a God-given Holy Land sounds from our pulpits, nor do we hear any clamor from our rank-and-file about the "sin" of relinquishing land to non-Jews. As outlined in *Emet ve-Emunah*, Conservative ideology nowhere deals directly with the Land of Israel as a theological mandate. Even where the subject is obliquely mentioned, the emphases are historical and covenantal.

> From time immemorial, Eretz Yisrael has played a central and vital role in the life and culture of world Jewry. The Bible indicates that God has promised the land of Israel to our ancestors and to their descendants. The *brit* (covenant) between God and the Jewish people created an unbreakable bond between us and the geographic entity we call Eretz Yisrael.[4]

> Our religion has been land-centered but never land-bound; it has been a portable religion so that despite our long exile (*galut*) from our spiritual homeland, we have been able to survive creatively and spiritually even in the *Tefutzot* (Diaspora).[5]

It is more difficult to dispel a suggested concern for ethical precepts in determining policy for peace, land, and security. But it is time we acknowledged that neither the right nor the left can claim sole possession of the "moral" position. Those on the right claim that their concern for the survival of our people is as much an ethical approach as the left's concern for peace. Their view has much validity, for survival certainly is a moral issue for us Jews. To acknowledge that is not to excuse the sometimes harsh and inhumane methods being employed in the occupied territories. Both the right and the left must demand ethical behavior by Jews and non-Jews in the Land of Israel, but neither must arrogate to itself the position of sole proprietor of "ethical behavior." Conservative Jews will only muddy the waters by making claims and counterclaims as to who is being *moral* to whom.

The third basic concern, that of security, is not simply a matter of achieving maximum protection. We are rather dealing with conflicting world views.

One of the two basic premises underlying the debate over security is: If we treat the Arab with respect and offer him civic responsibility, he will respond peacefully. This attitude posits that complex world problems are resolvable, that force of arms will not achieve a lasting peace, while education and humanitarian efforts will. This line of reasoning might lead us to withdraw from the territories and lead to a Palestinian state.

The other approach argues that man cannot be counted upon to respond positively to respect and responsibility, that there are certain problems which are nonresolvable. (Who, more than the Jew, knows that the world is cruel, unforgiving, and often unjust?) This position further states that those who have enjoyed a democratic upbringing have had a very special, but rare, life experience. The fears which emanate from this reasoning could lead us to annex unilaterally all the territories.

Were we to weigh the sum total of Jewish experience, the scales would likely be tipped toward pessimism. As Professor Salo Baron once noted, "Jewish history is a series of national tragedies strung together by our commemoration of them." Even if we were to call upon Jewish sources to defend the liberal optimism, we would be faced with confusing and contradictory quotes. Thus each optimistic liberal assumption could be balanced with a pessimistic illiberal one. For example: the idea that man is created in God's image (*zelem elohim*) and therefore his body is not to be intentionally disfigured or maimed; certainly not destroyed; could be juxtaposed by the biblical dictate that when a man rises to kill you, *hashkem vihargo,* quickly rise and kill him. Or similarly, the goodness of mankind as portrayed in the Bible could be pitted against the image of Amalek, that totally evil nation; or, the ultimate goal of creation by the fall of Adam and Eve after their sin in the Garden of Eden.

But clearly the time has come for decisive action. Israel can no longer maintain the status quo. The sabra has grown up and is asking not only "Can I exist in a hostile world?" but also "What kind of existence is worth sacrificing for?" We finally are reduced to asking: "What should Israel's face to the world be?"

There seems to be no choice left but to be "chosen" as best we can. But how? We must learn from our dreadful history so as not to repeat it. We also must sustain the optimistic view of Israel's fate, with all the energy we can muster, yet without a careless abandon that endangers us. Surely we must maintain a strong army while pursuing a negotiated peace.

A new Zionism is called for, one free of the once-legitimate concerns upon which the state was founded. We cannot bring up our children any longer with the siege mentality that was inescapable forty years ago. The old Zionism has failed to inspire the young Israeli leadership. Unless Zionism becomes more confident in the human potential for growth and bold in its efforts for peace, Israel will never achieve real security. We must choose the prophets of hope over the prophets of doom, lest our prophecies become self-fulfilling.

NOTES

1. Since this paper was written, the Kach Party has been outlawed in Israel as racist. However, two other right-wing parties, Tzomet and Moledet, hold similar positions.
2. Since this paper was written, the PLO meeting in Algiers, has declared an independent Palestinian state with predictable results: (1) the Arab countries recognize the new state; (2) the United States expresses support but does not recognize it; (3) the USSR recognizes it; (4) both Israel's major parties revile it.
3. Jordan's recent inactivity in the Israeli-Palestinian conflict suggests King Hussein's capitulation to Arafat.
4. *Emet ve-Emunah* (New York: Jewish Theological Seminary of America, Rabbinical Assembly, United Synagogue of America, Women's League for Conservative Judaism, and Federation of Jewish Men's Clubs, 1988), p. 37.
5. Ibid., p. 38.

The Israel Security Dilemma

JACOB STEIN

With remarkable prescience, the late Rabbi Abraham Joshua Heschel wrote more than twenty years ago:

> The Lord of history always placed us in predicaments and this seems to be part of our destiny. Never to relax in complacency, but to face difficult tasks. To live by the challenge. . . . the joy and exultation that come from Israel reborn are mixed with pain and chagrin over the suffering and bitterness that are found in the Middle East today.

Today, forty years after the rebirth of the state, Israel lives with an uncertain peace, its land without recognized borders and its security a heavy burden borne daily by its population. Challenging the central Zionist belief that Israel is, and must continue to be, a Jewish state are the almost two million Palestinian Arabs living in Israel and the occupied territories. Their birthrate far exceeds that of Israeli Jews, posing a serious demographic challenge to Israel's Jewish character and security.

The *intifada* (uprising in the territories) reflects a strong feeling of Palestinian nationalism. Ironically, the Palestinians' desire for their own homeland can be traced in part to the success of Zionism and the strength of the state it created. Yet when the United Nations voted for partition of Palestine in November 1947, most Arab states, and the Palestinian Arabs themselves, rejected this compromise, believing that the Palestinian state should be all of Palestine. Israel was established, the Palestinian Arabs were left without a state, and the war between them and Israel continues. It is a continuation of the Palestinian Arabs' war against the Jews started in the 1920s, internationalized as a conflict between Israel and Arab states in 1948, and now joined by the Palestinians resident in the territories.

The mass media have been fascinated by images of women and children throwing rocks and firebombs at Israeli tanks and armored vehicles, images that have raised the Palestinian problem to the forefront of international consciousness. Twenty years of efforts by Israel to build economic ties with the territories have been seriously weakened. There is a new awareness of the Green Line as Israel's border. Inevitably the seven hundred thousand Israeli Arabs are being drawn into and increasingly supporting the *intifada*, though largely through peaceful demonstrations to date (i.e., during 1988). Prospects for a settlement are dim. The hope of many Israelis that granting some form of autonomy to West Bank and Gaza Strip Palestinians would create conditions conducive to peace appears to be dashed.

A West Bank Palestinian–Jordanian delegation as a negotiating partner for Israel is not a real possibility. A new generation of Palestinians, no longer content to be "under the wing" of King Hussein, is demanding self-rule; its leaders came of age under Israeli occupation and do not know of the Jordanian rule from 1948 to 1967. Hanna Siniora, a prominent Palestinian newspaper editor, wrote in 1988, "If there is one message this uprising has made clear, it is that we do not want to parlay an occupation by Israel into domination by Jordan."

King Hussein may well not come to the negotiating table; his real interest is in ensuring his own survival. His July 1988 decision to sever legal and administrative ties to the West Bank and Gaza Strip, in effect ceding political control of the occupied territories, demonstrates this. However, he has insisted that Jordan's interests be considered in any settlement, and has not yet called for repeal of the 1950 law that unified the East and West Banks.

Many Palestinian nationalists draw strength from their Muslim faith, which views a Jewish state in their midst as a theological insult. Some depict Israel as a "thorn in the Arab flesh and a dagger pointed to the Muslim heart." Tens of thousands of West

Bank Jewish settlers, members of Gush Emunim, also reject compromise on the basis of religious beliefs. They are determined not to yield an inch of territory because the land supposedly is theirs by virtue of divine title. They believe that any concession or annulment of Israeli control of even the smallest part of their homeland and its transfer to a non-Jewish authority is absolutely prohibited by Torah and is simply the theft of land. These Jewish settlers may resist a decision to surrender any territory following a peace settlement. For many religious groups, returning territory is primarily a religious, not a political issue. When one's opinions represent absolute truth, there is no room for compromise, there is either truth or heresy. The nationalist parties who demand a "Greater Israel" support the settlers; going one step further are the Kahanists and their supporters, who call for the "transfer" of Arabs out of Israel and the territories. Thus, a good part of the Israeli population favors retaining the territories in their entirety.

But about half of Israel's population senses the danger of the status quo, and they believe that the 1967 war did not diminish basic Arab resources or change the balance of power in the Middle East. The Arabs far exceed Israel in territory, population, and wealth, and have the ability to say no to a settlement. Israel won the war but cannot dictate the peace, which will have to be negotiated.

A good part of the Arab world refuses to enter into meaningful negotiations with Israel. Despite its December 1988 overtures to the United States, the PLO refuses to abandon its Covenant calling for the liquidation of Israel. Yasir Arafat's new initiatives may yet be challenged and sabotaged by the Syrian and Iraqi wings of the PLO, as happened during the intra-PLO butchery in Lebanese refugee camps. A truly "moderate" resident Palestinian leadership would be a challenge to the PLO's power structure, and in the past, Arafat and PLO leaders have demonstrated that any West Bank and Gaza Palestinians who make "leadership" noises are quickly subject to a deadly response.

The one and one-half million Palestinians in the territories may yet join with their brothers in Jordan to take control of that country. If that happened, the dispute with Israel would continue, but it would be between the Palestinian state of Jordan and the

Jewish state of Israel. An argument over territory is subject to negotiation; a debate over one's national existence is not.

Thus, the elements for peace are not now present. The current Israeli political leadership appears unlikely to move towards peace, while many Arabs are convinced that time will reward them with what military initiatives have failed to achieve.

Thus, Israel must remain militarily strong and diplomatically resolute until it has leaders who command sufficient public confidence and popular support to make difficult compromises until Arab leaders decide, as Sadat did, that it is time to negotiate a settlement with the Jewish state.

Meanwhile, Israel should wage an intensive public relations campaign to present her case to the American people, press, and government. In 1948, Israel acquired arms from Czechoslovakia; in 1956, Mirage fighter aircraft from France. Today, Israel must rely almost exclusively on the United States to maintain its military strength. But American perceptions of Israel are changing from admiration and high regard for her moral values to concern over human rights violations and over the larger questions of Israel's continued occupation of the territories. Recent surveys confirm a marked decline in the number of Americans sympathetic to Israel. If permitted to grow unchallenged, these new perceptions can only benefit those seeking to weaken the American–Israeli link.

As American budgetary problems intensify, there will be increased questioning of the large-scale military and economic aid this country furnishes Israel. Jesse Jackson and other political leaders espousing third-world doctrines demanding Palestinian self-determination (and in some cases supporting the PLO) can seriously undermine congressional support of Israel.

To strengthen its case in Washington, Israel should be perceived as actively seeking peace, and should encourage American initiatives towards that end. For only the United States has been able to bring the conflicting parties to the table. No progress towards peace, whether a cease-fire, an armistice, or the 1979 peace treaty with Egypt, has ever been made without the personal involvement of the President and the Secretary of State.

Israel must be perceived as eschewing the suppression of another people, for it cannot continue to occupy territories inhabited by one and one-half million hostile Arabs without losing substantial American public support.

What of American Jewish public criticism of Israel? Clearly, peace, land, and security are issues whose resolution dramatically affect and may jeopardize Israeli lives. Decisions concerning them must be made by the Israelis themselves; our advice, when published in public forums generally is not helpful. American Jewish criticism of Israel lately has found a wider audience in the secular press. Generally, critical disagreement fails to address the historical context in which the issue must be understood. Whatever the nature of our remarks, we must be attentive to that context. In Israel, debate and criticism do not need to be placed in context; Israelis live the context.

Having myself offered some implied criticism, I also want my Israeli friends to appreciate the American Jewish depth of commitment to Israel's security during these last forty years. It has been our priority political concern. We are partners in Israel's rebirth, and we seek a country which has its political roots in the American system of democracy and its moral and ethical roots in Jewish values.

Israel is critically dependent on the political, military, and economic support of the Bush administration. We American Jews are a minority, but by participating in the political process with a greater intensity than the general population, we magnify our role and increase our influence.

For forty years, Israel has been a voice calling out again and again for peace. It demonstrated, in its agreement with Egypt, that peace brings great benefits to the parties. But for now, most Arab ears appear deaf to peace. As it says in Proverbs, "I am for peace, but when I speak, they are for war."

SUMMARY

1. After forty years, Israel still does not have peace or recognized borders with her neighbors.
2. The *intifada* is part of a continuing war against the Jews started in the 1920s, internationalized as a conflict between Israel and

the Arab states in 1948, and now joined by Palestinians in the territories.
3. The media are fascinated by images of women and children throwing firebombs and stones against armed soldiers and armored vehicles. These images have raised the consciousness of the world community to Israeli occupation of the West Bank and Gaza Strip.
4. Israel is not prepared to negotiate for peace. It lacks the leadership, as well as the public support, necessary for negotiations which will involve territorial compromise.
5. There is no Palestinian Arab leadership prepared to guarantee a peace with Israel.
6. Israel, while waiting for a qualified negotiating partner, must retain American political, economic, and military support.
7. A strong public relations campaign by Israel is needed to state her case to the American public, press, and government, to ensure the necessary continuing support of the United States. American support is eroding under the influence of reports and images from the occupied territories. This erosion must be reversed.

Israel Is Fighting for Her Life

JOSEPH P. STERNSTEIN

It is imperative first to briefly examine the ideological underpinnings of Zionism's conception of achieving "Peace, Land, and Security in the State of Israel."

Zionism postulated, as an indispensable *conditio sine qua non,* the aim of "restoring a people to its land and the land of its people." Whether we desire our National Jewish Homeland to be an epitome of *or la-goyim* ("a light unto the nations") or *kekhol ha-goyim* ("like unto other nations"), neither could be attained without the condition precedent of physical sovereignty in Eretz Yisrael.

Thus, we immediately confront the issue of power. Unavoidable is the twofold consideration of the effect of power: first, to understand how the responsibility of wielding power acts upon the collective psyche of the Jewish people, both within and without the State of Israel. Second, what effect does the possession of this Jewish power have on the stance of the international community of nations vis-à-vis the State of Israel, or *ma yomru ha-goyim* ("what will the world say")?

A subtle nuance has been inserted into this state of affairs: Oldtime anti-Semitism may not be fashionable in modern political parlance, but criticism, condemnation, and even vile vituperation vented on the State of Israel, in contradistinction to Jews, can be piously subsumed under the category of acceptable international political appraisal. The sanctimonious stance of the Soviet Union relative to Israel's military victories may be an extreme example, but there is also not absent the vehement criticism of ostensibly "friendly" countries, such as France or Italy. The Yiddish proverb roughly translated, "One can speak of the daughter, but the clear inference is the daughter-in-law."

To probe the first area of transformed relationships, namely the *inner* status of Jewish control of power in the State of Israel—even *Jewish* voices are not loath to pronounce viewpoints on the morality of the Jewish exercise of power as it is wielded in order to maintain security. It is a concept not to be cavalierly dismissed or denigrated as hysteria. Not since the days of the Second Commonwealth have we Jews possessed the luxury of simultaneously assuming autonomous responsibility for wielding power while at the same time being able to appraise, praise, or condemn the morality of such use.

While such a discussion can deteriorate into an intellectually fundamentalist slugfest—and it did so degenerate in the turbulent days of the destruction of the Second Commonwealth—reasonable people must think differently. Even though it is impossible to subtract the influence of fundamentalism from the current Jewish equation, it is hoped that perspective as to the pace of extremism will forestall its taking over the arena.

One final ideological note to be considered. I view the worldwide Jewish discussion of this subject, as our symposium is titled—even with the clause "in the State of Israel"—as a startling and somewhat ironic vindication of a cardinal element in the ideological pantheon of Zionistic values. It was Herzl who said: *"Wir sind ein Volk"*—"We are one people." Not only is the nexus of common identity clear and irrefragable, but the Jewish *apprehension* of this truth is the vindication of Zionism. Further, the willingness of Jews within and without Israel to talk to each other about the security of the state is, in my Zionist judgment, to be encouraged and intensified. (Parenthetically, may I anticipate an argument which I will subsequently submit, namely, that I know of no responsible leader, in Israel or the Diaspora, who is not prepared to exchange, consider, respect, and *even act upon* mutual discussion. What does sunder viewpoints is the method of such discussion. But more about this later.)

It is clear that the events in Israel since December 1987—what the Arabs call *intifada* (uprising) and what Israeli leaders call "civil insurrection"—have provoked profoundly serious repercussions. While it is, as of the date of this paper, quite premature to fully appraise the historical effects of these events, all would agree that they constitute one of the more serious situations confronting Israel in the forty years of its existence.

I submit, however, that it should also be clear that the internal conflicts swirling about these events are not absolutely unique in Israel's stormy history. The arguments concerning morality, humanitarianism, etc., are not new. One needs to cast one's historical eye backward to the very days of the birth of the state. Then, too, there were deep cleavages in the Jewish body politic as to how the fight for the state should be waged. It should not be forgotten that aspects of this political quarrel were fought out on exalted Zionist turf. It was between Weizmann, who was aghast at the methods advocated by David Ben-Gurion and Abba Hillel Silver in the battle against the nefarious policies of Great Britain, and the latter two, who demanded all-out war against the Colonial Office. Then, too, "morality" and "humanitarianism" were by-words of the day. Then, too, there were those Jews who felt that it was more important to join in the universal battle for India's independence than to join the "sectarian" fray for a Jewish state.

All agree, I am persuaded, with the thesis that the essential security of the state *qua* state must not be jeopardized. This having been said, there are then two questions: First, what substantively should be on the negotiating table? Second, how to mobilize the requisite political and strategical moral force needed to obtain the objective?

The first rubric itself resolves into two issues. Initially, at this point, the slogan "land for peace" obtrudes; following, or as some would say, concomitant with this, is the question of procedure: Yes "international conference" or no? (It should be noted that even on the latter issue, there are some nuances: none in Israel would object if the United States and the Soviet Union would jointly and *exclusively* convene such a meeting.)

During the various Arab-Israeli wars the strategy of Israel was implicitly understood, even if frequently too horrendous to articulate: the Arabs could absorb several defeats and still bounce back;

for Israel, one defeat would be fatal. Thus, the luxury of experimentation, of trial and error, of an irresponsible foray into an uncertain diplomatic future is historically denied it. For this reason, many Israeli military strategists were the most dovish in the possibly unilateral introduction of nuclear weapons into this Middle Eastern conflict: the reserve possibility of a second strike is, due to numerical and geographical size and demographic distribution of population, catastrophically unwise.

I must state my bottom-line at this time. I do not see any immediately foreseeable solution to the area's tension, and it is imperative that all of Israel's friends understand the bleakness of the situation. Hence, prodding Israel from the sidelines with long hortatory poles (the length of which ensures the physical inviolability of those wielding the prodding poles) can only result in a debacle. This grim prognosis may be unpalatable, yet, alas, I see no other immediate future.

Why? It is imperative not to fall prey to the adroit propagandistic legerdemain of Israel's opponents, who seek to argue that history began in 1967. Israel is an occupier, runs the sleight-of-hand message. Even more, Israel relishes this role of an occupier. Occupation and control of foreign-owned land and a victim population is reprehensible. What follows, in this logical-historical syllogism, is obvious. Therefore, in order to forestall this false description of alleged history, we must *never* weary of explaining events, even going back to 1948. Israel was never the aggressor, always the victim. Israel repeatedly offered the olive branch, always spurned.

I do not dwell at length on the internal conflicts of the Arab world—with the brooding and ominous spectre of Muslim fundamentalism hanging over the combatants—which impel the Arab countries to vie with each other in the assumption of extremist positions vis-à-vis Israel.

Prime Minister Shamir, surely not characterized by many—Jews or non-Jews—as the most malleable of statesmen (although, I suspect, more flexible than many give him credit for) has stated openly, clearly, and officially: "Everything is on the table" in face-to-face negotiations with Arab states or Palestinian Arabs.

Yet we hear so many voices urging Israel—seemingly possessed of so many invincible implements of modern warfare against a "hapless, yet heroic array of children"—to be courageous and initiate discussions. Before dealing with the question of Israel's negotiating partner, I wish to dispose of the argument challenging Israel's military might as it is deployed against these "innocent" youths. Again we fall into the trap set with skill by our enemies. While Israel—and the record, if fairly displayed, will demonstrate this—has inhibited itself in its response, almost always using lethal weapons only as a last resort, one must never forget that its full arsenal *must* be fully operational *at all times* in order to forestall rash and dangerous possibilities. Already we are reading reports that Syria, reequipped and retrained, is preparing another stab at Israel.

To return to the question of Israel's negotiating partner. While Hussein has sanctimoniously and self-righteously withdrawn from the table (and I share the conviction that he will return, in one way or another—the existence of another independent Arab state, Palestinian in nature, on his doorstep, is a danger too real to countenance), the spotlight has focused on the PLO. Forget for a moment the evil nature of the PLO—its Covenant is too well known for it to be taken seriously by decent observers. Can anyone accept the possibility of an inevitably irredentist state in Gaza (I leave aside Judea and Samaria for a subsequent analysis) in that pressure-cooker? Anyone who has seen Gaza readily understands the impossibility of its becoming a state within its present borders. Egypt rebuffed it. Hussein shies away. What then?

Judea and Samaria present a political picture of a different hue. I wish to quote a recognized Israeli military expert: "A memorandum submitted by Pentagon experts shortly afterward [the 1967 war] determined that control of the central mountain range of Judea and Samaria to a frontier well east of Jerusalem was essential to assure Israel's security." Even the Allon Plan—which in the view of many was flawed by a "pie-in-the-sky" hope that a Palestinian state would remain content to leave her military security in the hands of Israel—envisaged Israeli military control of the Judean mountain ranges.

Thus, we come full circle to the Arab unrest, call it what you will: *intifada* or civil insurrection. Whence shall their help come?

From the Arab states, which have repeatedly cast them off? From the PLO, who are hacking to pieces any Arab who dares to accommodate himself to Israel? They are angry and frustrated and resentful. But they say it again and again (and why are there Jews who persist in making them "liars"?): they wish to attain control of Hebron and Nablus, of Ramallah and Jenin, of Gaza City and Khan Yunis, and also—of Jaffa and Haifa, of Jerusalem and Tel Aviv. It is important not to stuff our ears as they say it. They mean it.

I am therefore not sanguine about the immediate future, and I do not see any alternative course which political reality can dictate. International Peace Conference? Let me quote again from the previously noted military expert: "Thus, for deterrence purposes, foreign guarantees are useful only as a subsidiary reinsurance in situations where Israel can defend itself without outside help. When really needed for survival they would prove worthless." Abba Hillel Silver, in the days of inexpressible agony, would proclaim to the Jewish world the words of the Psalmist: "Do not rely on princes, nor on the children of men in whom there is no salvation." With much faith in our own United States, do honest and clear-eyed observers truly believe that America would heroically and always stand by Israel's side in the teeth of the inevitable universal "ganging-up" on Israel?

We turn now to the nettlesome question of American (or world) Jewish "speaking out."

Let me begin by making one statement, the verity of which I firmly believe should be the basis of any discussion: *I believe Israel is fighting for her life.* I do not believe that the Arabs want peace. I believe that the Arabs believe that they can outlast us and that time is on their side. Call it paranoia or whatever, I am not ready to rely on the "goodwill" of the world. Is this hysterical? Is this fanatical extremism? Is this self-defeating irrationality? I do not think so. I am persuaded that these are sober and correct conclusions, from which practical lessons can be drawn.

Based upon these premises, I am of that school of Jewish opinion which maintains that going to the public press is profoundly injurious to our cause. I do not feel that we must dance to every tune played by the Israeli piper, nor do I accept the view that there must not be disagreement with actions taken by Israel.

Simply put, I feel that our disagreements can be vented with our Israeli colleagues, but they should be aired privately. Many of us have always been met with attention, care, and seriousness. I can personally testify to several issues wherein Israel changed its position after consultation with world Jewish leadership.

The problem resolves itself into the question of serious political injury to Israel. I recall a specific meeting with high officials of the State Department, where the opening statement by an important State Department official was the declaration that he was basing his structures against Israel upon quotations by American Jewish leadership. Such statements, therefore, were transformed and reshaped as a political weapon with which Israel was bludgeoned and flayed. *Hakhamim, hizaharu be-divreikhem* ("Sages, be circumspect in your utterances").

I wish to add a final note concerning morality, humanitarianism, spiritual values, etc. With luxuriant plenitude, "moralists" have hectored and lectured Israel. Yet, in our tradition, *safeguarding of life* is paramount (except for three extenuations). Aside from accepting the biased, distorted, and perverted half-truths spewed out by an irresponsible and frenzied media as they were cunningly manipulated by "young, innocent women and children," there is one overriding talmudic dictum, rooted firmly in Jewish ethics, which tells us: *Ha-ba le-hargekha, hashkem ve-hargeihu* ("If someone rises up to kill you, kill him first") (Talmud Berakhot).

I regret to conclude on this note. It is stark, grim, and desolate: Our enemies wish, literally, to kill us.

SUMMARY

The renewal of Zionism has invested the Jewish people with the challenge, opportunity, and responsibility for the use of power. Collective and national existence on a geographical area of territory thrusts upon those inhabiting that area the duty of maintaining peace and order.

The heterogeneity of the population in the State of Israel uniquely infuses the task of maintaining law and order with problems of profound difficulty. Israel, as the result of wars precipitated by her neighbors, is burdened by residual hatreds, frustrations, bitter collective passions—all vented with wild ferocity and venom. The battlepoint of these complexities is rendered ever more difficult by the insertion of seemingly "innocent" elements into the fray. Thus world opinion, while on the surface pro-Israel but subterraneously anti-Semitic, has turned with fury upon Israel.

For some outside of Israel, (and inside, too), recent events have proven to be upsetting, as they allege an erosion of values in the Israeli body politic. In many cases, blindly accepting as truth the depiction of events by a one-sided and sensationalist media, these Jews have publicly unleashed a torrent of criticism upon Israel. This publicly aired wave of denunciation, often couched in irresponsible verbiage, has been twisted into political weaponry against Israel.

It is my contention that, while private debate and discussion should by no means be stifled, it must nevertheless be conducted with a sense of responsibility as to where *public* debate will lead us.

Our basic responsibility is to educate ourselves, train ourselves, and teach ourselves never to lose sight of the basic historical principles involved.

I am convinced that "we are fighting for our life" and therefore the framework and parameters of our thought and expression must be ordered congruent to the perception of responsibility.

The Necessity of Aiding Israel's Progressive Elements

LEON WALDMAN

The seizure of lands in the 1967 war created a situation appropriately termed by Professor Yeshayahu Leibowitz as "colonialism"—the relationship of "ruler and ruled." Invariably, such a situation leads to the exploitation of one people by the other and the diminishing of human dignity (both of the ruled and the ruler). As the people experiencing exploitation struggles to throw off the yoke of occupation, a stage we are now witnessing, violence and bloodshed inevitably occur.

Undeniably, 1.5 million Arabs do not wish to be under Israeli rule. The continued occupation of a large population of sullen and hostile Arabs has had a corrosive effect on Israel's social fabric and has exacted an enormous price in terms of the country's moral and spiritual capital. A way must be found for Israel to extricate herself from this morally unsavory situation.

Some say, "Would that we could but the territories are necessary for security." The greatest military threat to Israel is from the standing armies of the neighboring Arab states. Once it was believed that Israeli control of the West Bank provided a buffer against the possible thrust of Arab armies across the country's midsection. Now, a growing body of expert opinion believes that advances in technology (e.g., demilitarization of the West Bank, forward listening posts and intelligence stations, and AWACs surveillance), and Israel's vastly superior military capabilities create the possibility for territorial compromise which will not compromise Israel's security in the least.

Of course, such matters, being highly technical, are best left to the experts, who will supply important information about where international borders can be drawn and under what conditions. It is enough to state that a growing number of Israel's military strategists, army officers, scientists, and political leaders believe the territories are *not* a security imperative!

The occupied territories, in fact, sap the strength of Israel's armed forces by (1) requiring soldiers to act as policemen in controlling a huge civilian population (many experts believe that Israel's Defense Forces would better be able to defend Israel were they not deployed in the territories chasing women and children down alleys) and (2) creating a military obligation to protect dozens of Jewish settlements in the midst of hostile Arabs.

The corrupting effect of the occupation, the nonstrategic value of the territories, and the fact that they are military liabilities, make it imperative for Israel to end the occupation and move towards peace with its Arab neighbors.

Some cast the debate over Israel's security as between those who are "naive," who would imperil Israel's existence by compromising her territorial security, and those who are "realistic" about Arab motives and character, and therefore correctly resist the idea of land for peace. I agree that Israel's security and existence are paramount, and that Israel would be foolish to rely on Arab goodwill and promises.

Israel can rely only on ironclad agreements which she herself can adequately police and enforce. No border should be drawn except along lines dictated by the best, most tough-minded military strategic planners.

Two groups oppose territorial compromise for peace.

1. *Secular ultranationalists,* with their grandiose dreams of a Greater Israel stretching from the Euphrates to the Nile, and, like the Great Powers, of a sphere of influence beyond. The ultranationalist program calls for ending Israel's rule over the Arabs in the territories not by withdrawal but by annexing the territories and then "transferring" the Arabs. What was once regarded as talk of the lunatic Kahane fringe has appeared with increasing frequency

amid the nationalist camp, with the softening touches of euphemism (e.g., "an exchange of population").

We have already witnessed the dangers of such self-delusion when, in 1982, Israel's Minister of Defence and Chief of Staff, both known for their ultranationalist views, tried to rearrange the political map of Lebanon with catastrophic results. Ultranationalist ideas, particularly transfer, are repugnant to many of us, not least because of our people's experience in this century.

2. *Religious nationalists,* including fundamentalists, messianists, and apocalyptics whose goal is the establishment of a theocracy in Israel. They ascribe to the land a measure of sanctity bordering on idolatry. While many in this group endorse transfer, such a drastic move would be unnecessary because Arab residents of the annexed lands would not be granted Israeli citizenship or other rights. Rather, they would become permanent "hewers of wood and drawers of water."

These two groups share a disdain for values which characterize the Western political tradition. To the Jewish people's shame, a number of leading government officials, including leading religious figures, have made public statements reflecting complete contempt for democratic values, pluralism, egalitarianism, equal justice for all (regardless of nationality or religion), and the primacy of the rule of law.

Thus, the debate about peace, land, and security in the State of Israel is really about the basic vision of the Jewish state.

As Conservative Jews, we have something special to contribute to this debate. We have strong attachments to our teachings, traditions, and history, and also have deep feelings for the values of the political experiment called America. We represent a unique synergy of values created by two traditions which stress the sanctity of life and the dignity of man.

We should strongly identify with and help advance those forces in Israeli life—movements, organizations, even political parties—which affirm the democratic and authentically Jewish values most precious to us. Our means of doing so might include:

- Providing direct financial assistance.
- Using the Israeli media to publicize our support.

- Inviting Israeli leaders with views congruent to the ones espoused above to our synagogues.
- Acting as education centers for this particular Zionist point of view, so as to help disseminate its message to the larger American community.
- Placing articles and advertisements in the American press identifying with the progressive, democratic elements in Israeli life.
- Championing this position in the internal debates of the American Jewish community rather than permitting the most hawkish elements to shape policy under the guise of security.

Contributors

DR. RAPHAEL ARZT

Associate dean of the Seminary of Judaic Studies in Jerusalem and director of its TALI Education Fund, Dr. Arzt has served on the founding board of trustees of the Masorti movement and has written extensively on the field of Jewish education. He is a former director of Camp Ramah in Connecticut/New England.

SHOSHANAH CARDIN

President of the National Conference on Soviet Jewry since the Fall of 1988, Mrs. Cardin is a past president of the Council of Jewish Federations and currently sits on the board of governors of the Jewish Agency. She has given special attention to the responsibilities of lay leaders in confronting Israel/Diaspora issues.

DR. STEVEN M. COHEN

Professor of sociology at Queens College and a visiting professor at the Jewish Theological Seminary of America, Dr. Cohen is co-author of two books to be published in 1990: *Two Worlds of Judaism: The Israeli and American Experiences* and *Cosmopolitan Parochials: Modern Orthodox Jews in America*. His most recent book is *American Assimilation or Jewish Revival?*

RABBI PAUL FREEDMAN

Director of the United Synagogue Youth's Departments of Israeli Affairs and Youth Activities, and leader of USY's Israel Pilgrimage, Rabbi Freedman also serves as coordinator of the Conservative movement's Settlement Committee.

JAC FRIEDGUT

A financial expert and a former Vice-president of New York's Citibank, Mr. Friedgut was a previously Vice-chairman of the National United Synagogue Committee on Israel. He now lives in Israel where he is President of Congregation Moreshet Avraham in Jerusalem's East Talpiot.

RABBI NEIL GILLMAN

Associate Professor of Jewish Philosophy at the Jewish Theological Seminary of America, Rabbi Gillman is the author of *Sacred Fragments: Exploring Jewish Theology,* published in early 1990. He has written extensively on the place of ritual and liturgy in Judaism, modern Jewish theology, and the ideology of the Conservative movement.

DR. DAVID GORDIS

Vice-president of the University of Judaism in Los Angeles and Director of the Susan and David Wilstein Institute of Jewish Policy, Dr. Gordis formerly served as executive vice-president of the American Jewish Committee.

DR. MOSHE GREENBERG

Professor of Bible at the Hebrew University, with a special interest in biblical law and the history of Bible interpretation, Dr. Greenberg helped fashion the Bible curriculum of Israel's public schools. He is associated with the Masorti movement's Seminary of Judaic Studies.

RABBI REUVEN HAMMER

Professor in the department of rabbinics at the Jerusalem campus of the Jewish Theological Seminary of America, Rabbi Hammer also is a visiting professor at the Seminario Rabinico Latinoamericano in Buenos Aires. Currently president of the Rabbinical Assembly of Israel, he is author of *The Other Child in Jewish Education* and translator of *Sifre: A Tannaitic Commentary on the Book of Deuteronomy.*

DR. PAULA HYMAN

Lucy Moses Professor of Modern Jewish History at Yale University, Dr. Hyman was dean of the Seminary College of Jewish Studies (JTSA) from 1981 to 1986. Her most recent book is *The Jewish Family: Myth and Reality,* co-edited with Steven M. Cohen.

DR. LEE I. LEVINE

Vice-Chancellor of Israel Affairs at the Jewish Theological Seminary of America, Dr. Levine also is dean of the Seminary of Judaic Studies in Jerusalem and professor of archeology at the Hebrew University.

DR. DAVID LIEBER

A vice-chancellor of the Jewish Theological Seminary of America, Dr. Lieber is president of the University of Judaism and its Skovron Distinguished Service Professor. A specialist in biblical literature and thought, he also teaches in the Department of Near Eastern Languages at UCLA.

DR. CHARLES LIEBMAN

Professor of political science at Bar Ilan University in Israel, Dr, Liebman is the author of many studies of American Jews and of religion and politics in Israel.

RABBI STANLEY RABINOWITZ

A past president of the Rabbinical Assembly, Rabbi Rabinowitz was founding president of Mercaz: The Movement to Reaffirm Conservative Zionism from 1978 to 1982. He was senior rabbi at Congregation Adas Israel in Washington, D.C. from 1960 to 1986 and currently serves as its rabbi emeritus.

DR. ISMAR SCHORSCH

Chancellor of the Jewish Theological Seminary of America, Dr. Schorsch is also the Seminary's Rabbi Herman Abramowitz Professor of Jewish history.

RABBI BENJAMIN J. SEGAL

Director of the Ramah Programs in Israel, Rabbi Segal is the author of *Returning: The Land of Israel in Jewish History,* as well as of numerous articles on Israel, the Bible, midrash and Jewish education.

BARBARA SPECTRE

Chairperson of the Seminary of Judaic Studies' board of directors since the Seminary's inception (1984), Mrs. Spectre also is a lecturer in Judaic Studies at the Hebrew University's Melton Centre, the Yellin Teacher's College (Jerusalem) and the Achvah Teachers' Seminary (Be'er Tuvia).

RABBI PHILIP SPECTRE

Executive Director of the Masorti Movement in Israel, Rabbi-Spectre served for 15 years as spiritual leader of Congregation Netzach Israel in Ashkelon following his making aliyah in 1966.

JACOB STEIN

An active real estate investor and land developer, Mr. Stein was special advisor of the White House during the Reagan Administration. He also is a member of the commission which produced *Emet v'Emunah,* the Conservative statement of philosophy, as well as former chairman of the Conference of Presidents of Major American Jewish Organizations and a former president of the United Synagogue of America.

DR. GAD UFAZ

A lecturer in the department of Jewish thought at Oranim, Dr. Ufaz specializes in the thought of *chalutzic* (pioneer) Zionism. He also is a member of Kibbutz Ayelet Hashachar and of the "Shedemot Circle" (*Shedemot* is the kibbutz cultural periodical).

RABBI LEON WALDMAN

Spiritual leader of Congregation Beth El in Fairfield, Conn., Rabbi Waldman has extensive experience planning and leading interfaith and study missions to Israel. He has taught courses on Jewish history and Jewish thought at Fairfield University and currently chairs the Commission on Community Relations of The Greater Bridgeport Jewish Federation.

RABBI JOSEPH S. WERNIK

Chairman of the Organization Department of the World Zionist Organization (WZO), Rabbi Wernik served for ten years as national executive director of the Association of Americans and Canadians in Israel. He currently is a member of the WZO Executive and of the Jewish Agency's board of governors, and is immediate past president of the Masorti movement in Israel.

The Co-Editors

DR. JOHN RUSKAY

Vice-Chancellor for public affairs at the Jewish Theological Seminary of America, Dr. Ruskay formerly served as education director of the 92nd Street YMHA in New York.

DAVID M. SZONYI

Director of the Jewish Foundation for Christian Rescuers, a project of the Anti-Defamation league, Mr. Szonyi also is a practicing psychotherapist. He is former associate director of the Radius Institute and edited *The Holocaust: An Annotated Bibliography and Resource Guide*.

Participants in Zionism Conference September 7th and 8th, 1988

ABBREVIATIONS INDICATING ORGANIZATIONAL AFFILIATION

CA	Cantors Assembly
GN	Garin Nitzan
JEA	Jewish Educators Assembly
JNF	Jewish National Fund
JTS	Jewish Theological Seminary
JTS-Stud	Jewish Theological Seminary Student
MAS	Foundation for Masorti Judaism in Israel
FJMC	Federation of Jewish Men's Clubs
Mercaz	Mercaz
Ometz	Ometz
P	Presenter
RA	Rabbinical Assembly
Ramah	National Ramah Commission
UJ	University of Judaism
US	United Synagogue
USY	United Synagogue Youth
WCS	World Council of Synagogues
WL	Women's League for Conservative Judaism
WZO	World Zionist Organization

INDIVIDUAL PARTICIPANTS

William Abrams (Mercaz)
Dr. Robert Abramson (US)
Caryn Adelman (MAS)
Dr. Jerome Agrest (FJMC)

Motti Arad (Mercaz)
Rabbi Raphael Arzt (P)
Evelyn Auerbach (WL)

Bernice Balter (WL)
Rabbi Shlomo Balter (WCS)
Alan Bandler (MC)
Bernard Barsky (WCS)
William Batkay (Mercaz)
David Berkman (JTS-Stud)
Cheryl Birkner (Ometz)
Shmuel Birnham (JTS-Stud)
Leonardo Bitran (GN)
Rabbi Alan Blaine (RA)
Herschel Blumberg (JTS)
Kenneth Bravo (FJMC)

Shoshana Cardin (P)
Audrey Citak (WCS)
Burton Citak (US)
Rabbi Marim Charry (JEA)
Roy Clements (US)
Dr. Gerson D. Cohen (JTS)
Joyce Arnoff Cohen (JTS)
Dr. Steven A. Cohen (P)

Dr. Aryeh Davidson (JTS)
Rabbi Sheldon Dorph (UJ)

Ted Eisenberg (FJMC)
Rabbi Jerome Epstein (US)
Sylvia Ettenberg (JTS)
Len Feiwus (JTS-Stud)
Rabbi Ezra Finkelstein (RA)
Dr. Hertzl Fishman (MAS)
Rabbi Paul Freedman (P)
Rabbi Wayne Franklin (RA)
Jac Friedgut (P)

Judge Abraham Gafni (Mercaz)
Miriam Gafni (Mercaz)
Yaakov Gali (WZO)
David Geffen (MAS)
Alvin Gershen (WCS)
Elana L. Gershen (Mercaz)
Dr. Neil Gillman (P)
Rabbi Simon Glustrom (WCS)

Barbara Goldfarb (WL)
Dr. Solomon Goldman (JNF)
Helen Kirshblum Goldstein (WCS)
Dr. David Gordis (P)
Rabbi Michael Greenbaum (JTS)
Dr. Moshe Greenberg (P)
Dr. Simon Greenberg (JTS)
Alice Greenfield (MAS)
Dr. Edward Greenstein (JTS)

Phyllis Haas (WL)
Rabbi Reuven Hammer (P)
Rabbi Richard Hammerman (RA)
Rabbi Eliezar Havivi (MAS)
Heidi Heft (MAS)
Harold M. Helfman (FJMC)
Lynn Heller (WL)
Evelyn Henkind (JTS)
Jack M. Herman (FJMC)
Mildred Holtzman (US)
Jason Horn (US)
Rabbi William Horn (RA)
Dr. Paula Hyman (P)

Tom Kagedan (US)
Harry S. Katz (US)
Dr. Marvin Keller (US)

Participants in Zionism Conference

Hazzan Robert Kieval (CA)
Hindy Kisch (Mercaz)
Rabbi David C. Kogen (JTS)
Rabbi Benjamin Z. Kreitman (US)
Elaine Kremens (MAS)
William Kremens (MAS)
Goldie Kweller (WCS)

Rabbi William Lebeau (JTS)
Penny Leifer (WL)
Rabbi Morton Leifman (JTS)
Dr. Anne L. Lerner (JTS)
Bruce J. Leson (FJMC)
Arthur Levine (Mercaz)
Dr. David Lieber (P)
Dr. Charles Liebman (P)
Norman Lipoff (MAS)
Riva Gershen Lowy (Ramah)

Samuel Mansky (Mercaz)
Benjamin Margolis (JEA)
Blanche Meisel (WL)
Lou Meltzer (WCS)
Hazzan Solomon Mendelson (CA)
Rabbi Jeremy Milgrom (MAS)
Rabbi Michael Monson (MAS)
Ron Muroff (JTS-Stud)

Rabbi Judah Nadich (RA)
Moshe Nativ (WZO)
J. Harold Nissen (FJMC)
Neil Norry (MAS)

Larry Oxenberg (Mercaz)
Stephen M. Peck (JTS)
Deborah Perla (JTS-Stud)
Deborah Perlow (MAS)

Dr. Mayer Rabinowitz (JTS)
Rabbi Stanley Rabinowitz (P)
Einat Ramon (JTS-Stud)
Rabbi Perry Rank (RA)
Irving Robbin (Ramah)
Ruth Rosenfeld (WL)
Rabbi Jack Rosoff (RA)
Melvin Ross (JTS)
Dr. John Ruskay (JTS)

Elaine Schanzer (WL)
Jon Schechter (JTS-Stud)
James Schlesinger (MAS)
Evelyn Seelig (WL)
Marvin Selter (FJMC)
Robert Seltzer (FJMC)
Henry Sender (WCS)
Miriam Klein Shapiro (JEA)
Dr. Saul Shapiro (US)
Rabbi Alan Silverstein (RA)
Rabbi Charles Simon (FJMC)
Rabbi Gerald Skolnik (RA)
Barbara Spectre (P)
Rabbi Philip Spectre (P)
Jacob Stein (P)
Rabbi Joseph Sternstein (P)

Jennifer Tescher (USY)
Rabbi Richard Thaler (RA)
Alan Tichnor (MAS)
Janet Tobin (WL)
Rabbi Moshe Tutnauer (MAS)

Dr. Gad Ufaz (P)

Dr. Richard Wagner (JEA)
Rabbi Leon Waldman (P)
Selma Weintraub (WCS)

Rabbi Joseph Wernik (P) Martin Zuckerbrod (FJMC)
Marshall Wolke (WCS) Debbie Zuckerman (Ramah)

Conference Program

Zionism and Zionist Thought Within the Conservative/Masorti Movement: Deepening Our Commitment

A two-day closed conference for Conservative Movement leadership, convened by Chancellor Ismar Schorsch, in cooperation with the United Synagogue, Rabbinical Assembly, Women's League for Conservative Judaism, Federation of Jewish Men's Clubs, World Council of Synagogues, Mercaz, the Foundation for Conservative Judaism in Israel, the Masorti Movement, the University of Judaism, and the Jewish Theological Seminary.

SEPTEMBER 7–8, 1988

Wednesday, September 7, 1988

10:00 a.m.	Conference Opening Session Chairman—Simon Schwartz Address—"Israel: A Light Unto the Nations"—Ismar Schorsch
11:00 a.m.–1:00 p.m.	Seminar Session I *Seminar 1*—Democratic Values in the State of Israel Chairperson—Neil Norry Presenters—Shoshana Cardin, David Gordis, Barbara Spectre, Gad Ufaz Resource Person—Bernice Balter

Seminar 2—Israel-Diaspora Relations

Chairperson—Jerome Agrest
Presenters—Raphael Arzt, Steven M. Cohen, Paul Freedman, David Lieber
Resource Person—Michael Monson

Seminar 3—The Role of Religion in Israel

Chairperson—Evelyn Auerbach
Presenters—Charles Liebman, Stanley Rabinowitz
Resource Person—Charles Simon

Seminar 4—Aliyah

Chairperson—Marshall Wolke
Presenters—Jac Friedgut, Paula Hyman, Benjamin Segal, Joseph Wernik
Resource Person—Tom Kagedan

Seminar 5—The Centrality of the State of Israel in Jewish Life

Chairperson—Evelyn Henkind
Presenters—Neil Gillman, Moshe Greenberg, Reuven Hammer
Resource Person—Hindi Kisch

Seminar 6—Peace, Land and Security in the State of Israel

Chairperson—Miriam Gafni
Presenters—Philip Spectre, Jacob Stein, Joseph Sternstein, Leon Waldman
Resource Person—Bernard Barsky

1:00–2:00 p.m.	Informal Luncheon
2:15–5:45 p.m.	Seminar Session II
6:00–6:30 p.m.	Reception

Conference Program

6:30–8:00 p.m.	Conference Dinner Chairperson—Stephen M. Peck Presentation—"The Meaning of Zionism for Masorti Jews in the 21st Century"—Lee Levine
8:15 p.m.	Seminar Session III (if needed).

Thursday, September 8

9:15 a.m.–12:30 p.m.	Plenary Session I—Franklin Kreutzer, presiding
12:30–1:15 p.m.	Luncheon
1:30–4:15 p.m.	Plenary Session II—continued reports of Seminars Albert Lewis, presiding
4:15–4:45 p.m.	Coffee break
4:45–6:00 p.m.	Concluding Session—Ismar Schorsch, presiding Comments—Joseph Wernik General discussion reviewing conference, interim decisions regarding future efforts.

Index

Abrams, Morris, 72
Ahad Ha-Am, 18, 148
Akiva, on the dignity of man, 42
Aliyah: *see* Migration
Alkalay, Yehuda, 7
Allon, Yigal, 5–6; "Education for Humanity in Time of War," 5
Aloni, Shulamit, 79
Anti-Semitism in State of Israel, 79–86
Arafat, Yasir, 167
Auto-emancipation (Pinsker), 17
Avineri, Shlomo, 71
Awad, Mubarak, 93

Barak, Aharon, 21
Baron, Salo, 163
Barzel, Alexander, 120
Begin, Menahem, 5, 55, 62
Ben Azzi, 42
Ben-Gurion, David, 21–22, 55, 173
Berlin, Meir, 89
Buber, Martin, *On Zion: The History of an Idea*, 33–34

Camp David Agreement, 159
Church and state in State of Israel, 25–31, 38–39; defining role of religion in the state, 79–86; diaspora and State of Israel, 75; Orthodoxy and modernity, 139
Civil rights, 59–66; and gentiles, 17–22
Cohen, Zadoc, 87

Conservative Judaism, migration to Israel, 97–110; in shaping of the State of Israel, 7–14
Council of Jewish Federations, 12
The Counterlife (Roth), 105

Davis, Moshe, 123
Diaspora, bridging gap with State of Israel, 71–76; church and state issue, 75; decision making in State of Israel, 25–31; fear of rupture in State of Israel, 3; Israeli consciousness, 67–70; Israeli relations, 59–66; mutual interests with State of Israel, 122–23

Education: cultural development in State of Israel, 111–17; Jewish education, 39–40
"Education for Humanity in Time of War," (Allon), 5
Einstein, Albert, 1
Eisen, Arnold, 122–23
Eliade, Mircea, 129
Eliezer, 44
Equal rights and State of Israel, 18–22, 42, 45, 59–66
Ethiopean Jews, 10, 20

Frankel, Zacharias, 1, 7, 147
Free choice of religion, 25–31, 59–66, 75
Friedlander, Israel, 148

Geertz, Clifford, 129
Gentiles, 28–30; civil rights, 17–22
Goldstein, Israel, 111
Graetz, Heinrich, 1
Greenberg, Simon, 111

Ha-Aretz, 46, 79
Halkin, Hillel, 148
Halkin, Simon, 121
Hauser, Rita, 72
Hebrew language, 19, 108
Hertzberg, Arthur, 121
Herzl, Theodor, 1, 18, 45, 87, 147, 172
Heschel, Abraham Joshua, 2, 10, 148–50, 165; *Israel,* 148, 150
Hess, Moses, 7
Hussein, King, 160, 162, 166, 175

Intifada, 3–4, 31, 165–66, 169, 173, 175
Israel (Heschel), 148, 150
Israeli Communist Party, 35

Jackson, Jesse, 169
Jerusalem Post, 79
Jewish Agency, 11, 65, 68; and cultural development in State of Israel, 21–22
Jewish homeland and Judaism, 147–56
Joint Distribution Committee, 12
Jordan/Palestinian State, 160–61
Judaism: democratic values in State of Israel, 42–45; and Jewish homeland, 147–56; national character of Judaism, 1

Kach Party, 35, 159
Kadushin, Max, 54
Kahane, Meir, 3, 10, 62, 180
Kalischer, Zvi, 7
Kaplan, Mordecai, 75–76
Karo, Joseph, 88
Keren, Hayesod, 12
Kook, Rav, 83

Law of Return, 2, 26, 84, 89–90, 92–93, 150
Leeser, Isaac, 7
Leibowitz, Yeshayahu, 88, 179
Le Pen, Jean Marie, 3
Levinger, Miriam, 46
Likud Party, 159–60
Los Angeles Times, 60

Maimon, Fishman, 89
Maimonides, 150
Mapam Party, 159
Mendelssohn, Moses, 6
Messianism, 28–30
Migration to State of Israel: American Jewish community, 121–22; Conservative Judaists, 97–110; education and cultural development, 111–17; Ethiopean immigrants, 10; mutual interests of Israel and diaspora, 122–23; problems of settlement in State of Israel, 97–104; rabbinical students year-long stay in Israel, 115–16; State of Israel and Jewish life, 119–25
Myth and Reason in Contemporary Judaism (Tal), 47

Nachmanides, 150
National Religious Party, 35–36
Neturei Karta, 35, 139

On Zion: The History of an Idea (Buber), 33–34
Orthodox Judaism: freedom of religious choice in State of Israel, 25–31; growth of power in Israel, 2–6; messianism, 28–30; role of religion in State of Israel, 79–86

Palestine Liberation Organization, 4, 7–14, 167–68, 175–76
Palestiniean State, 160–61
Peres, Shimon, 62, 64
Pinsker, Leo, *Auto-emancipation,* 17

Index

Rabbinate, year-long Israel stay for rabbinical students, 115–16
Rabi, Yaacov, 80
Ratz Party, 159
Religious freedom: *see* Church and state
Riskin, Shlomo, 100
Rosenzweig, Franz, 150
Rotenstreich, Nathan, 74, 122
Roth, Philip, *The Counterlife,* 105

Sabbath observance, 17, 38
Sadat, Anwar, 168
Schechter, Solomon, 147–48
Schindler, Alexander, 72
Schweid, Eliezer, 120
Sephardic communities in State of Israel, 20
Sharon, Ariel, 62
Shulhan Arukh, 87–88
Silver, Abba Hillel, 173, 176
Simon, Ernst, 4
Siniora, Hanna, 166
State of Israel: church and state issue, 25–31, 38–39, 75, 139; civil rights, 17–22, 59–66; communal settlements, 55–56; cultural development, 111–17; Declaration of Independence and equal rights, 18–22, 42; defense of territory, 165–70; democratic prospects, 45–46; election procedures, 21–22; equal rights, 18–22, 42, 45, 59–66; Ethiopean Jews, 10, 20; freedom of religious choice, 25–31; gentiles, 17–22, 28–30; halakhic regimen, 87–94; Hebrew as official language, 19; homeland derived from piety and justice, 5; *Intifada,* 3–4, 31, 165–66, 169, 173, 175; Israeli Independence Day, 153; Jewish education, 39–40; Judaism and democratic values, 42–45; leadership of rabbinate and laity, 8; military service, 2; modernization by religious and secular leadership, 9; Orthodox Judaism, 2–6, 25–31, 79–96; peace and new Zionism, 159–64; pluralistic society, need for, 1–6; relations with diaspora, 59–66; religious nationalists, 181; role of religion in state, 79–86; Sabbath observances, 17, 38; ultra-nationalism, 179–82; unifying forces, 2; westernization, fear of, 19
Stranger at the Gate and gentile relationships, 29–30

Tal, Uriel, *Myth and Reason in Contemporary Judaism,* 47
Techiya Party, 159
31st Zionist Congress, 1
Torah as writ for democracy, 43
Tradition, diaspora and relations with State of Israel, 79–86

United Jewish Appeal, 12, 59, 63–65
United Nations and State of Israel, 4–6
Urbach, Ephraim, 121
Ussishkin, Menahem, 1

Weinfeld, M., 149
Weizmann, Chaim, 55, 173
World Jewish Congress, 12
World Zionist Congress, 64
World Zionist Organization, 1, 11–12, 68, 93, 119, 124

Yehoshua, 44
Yohanan ben Zakkai, 43, 54–56

Zionism, 54–57; ideological considerations, 53–54; independence of State of Israel and world opinion, 25–31